United Arab Emirates

United Arab Emirates

BY BYRON AUGUSTIN

Enchantment of the World
Second Series

138113

Children's Press®

A Division of Scholastic Inc.

NEW YORK   TORONTO   LONDON   AUCKLAND   SYDNEY
MEXICO CITY   NEW DELHI   HONG KONG
DANBURY, CONNECTICUT

Frontispiece: Marble replica of the Qur'an at Sharjah

Consultant: Dr. John Duke Anthony, CEO & President, The National Council
for U.S./Arab Relations, Washington, D.C.

Please note: All statistics are as up-to-date as possible at the time of publication.

Book Production by Herman Adler Design

Library of Congress Cataloging-in-Publication Data

Augustin, Byron.
    United Arab Emirates / by Byron Augustin.
        p. cm. — (Enchantment of the world. Second series)
    Includes bibliographical references and index.
    ISBN 0-516-20473-4
    1. United Arab Emirates—Juvenile literature. [1. United Arab Emirates.]
    I. Title. II. Series.
    DS247.T8 A94 2002
    953.57—dc21   00-065958

Acknowledgments

I would like to acknowledge my wife, Rebecca, who supported this project with patience and understanding, and who also edited the text. I am thankful to Dr. John Duke Anthony for introducing me to the Arab world. Dr. Edmund Ghareeb, of the Embassy of the United Arab Emirates, provided unwavering support throughout the project. I am extremely grateful to Dr. Ibrahim al-Abed, of the Ministry of Information and Culture in Abu Dhabi, for his assistance in arranging my research visit. A warm note of thanks is offered to Obaid al-Mutawa who introduced me to his father and the charming village of Aseema. I extend a final note of gratitude to all of the officials and people of the United Arab Emirates who provided true hospitality to a stranger.

This book is dedicated to Sheikh Zayed bin Sultan al-Nahyan; Rebecca, Andrew, Kelly, and Mark; and the Arabs.

Contents

Cover photo:
A boy and
his camels

Desert sand dunes

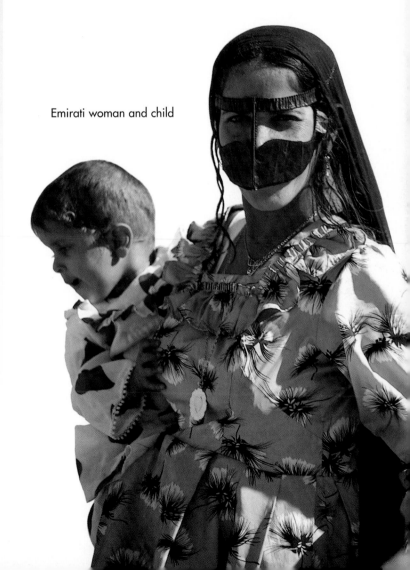

Emirati woman and child

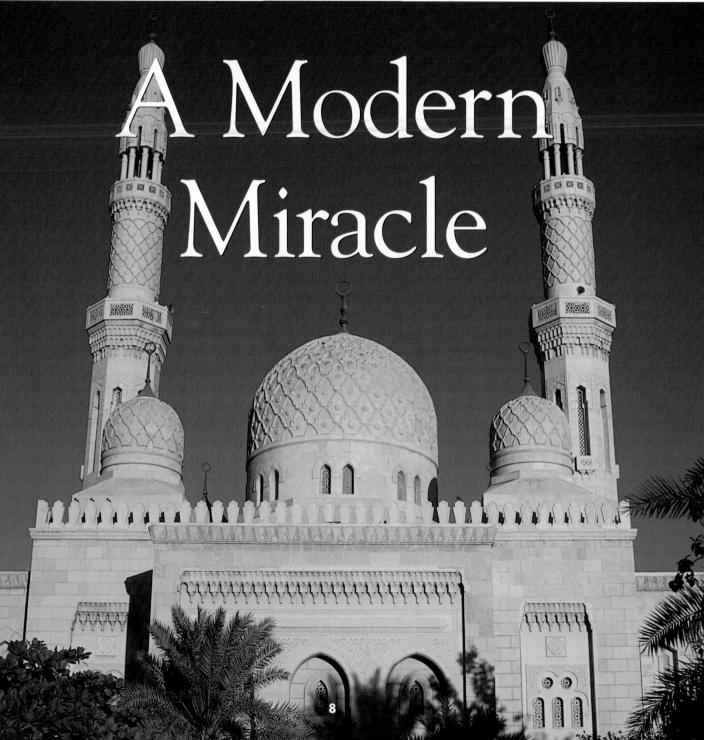

A Modern Miracle

Sand dunes in the desert

FOR CENTURIES, WINDS WHIPPED ACROSS THE DESERTS OF eastern Arabia. Sand moved with the wind, shaping dunes that looked like the waves of an ocean. Occasionally, a Bedouin tribe brought goats or other animals in search of vegetation. Then, like a mirage, they were gone. It was impossible for them to know that below the sand lay inconceivable wealth. Vast pools of oil and gas would be discovered in the future. The income from those energy resources would be used to shape a new nation—the United Arab Emirates (UAE).

Outside Influence

The land that is now included in the United Arab Emirates has been occupied by humans for a very long time. The country's geographical location has made it a crossroads for many

Opposite: **Jumeriah Mosque**

Geopolitical map of the
United Arab Emirates

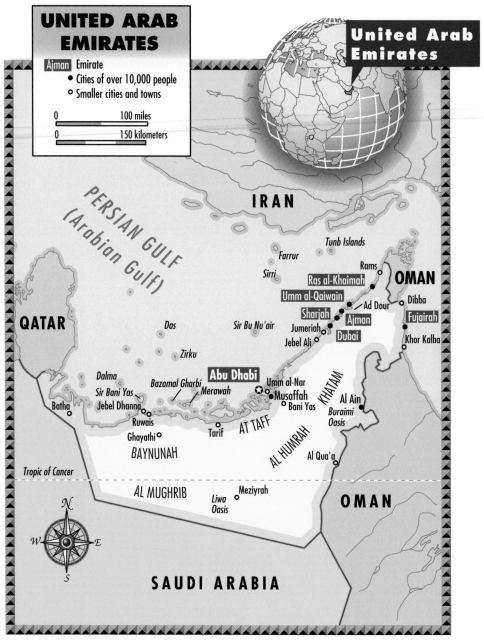

UNITED ARAB EMIRATES

Ajman Emirate
- Cities of over 10,000 people
○ Smaller cities and towns

0 _____ 100 miles
0 _____ 150 kilometers

United Arab Emirates

PERSIAN GULF
(Arabian Gulf)

IRAN

Tunb Islands

Farrur

Sirri

Rams

Ras al-Khaimah

OMAN

Umm al-Qaiwain

Dibba

Ad Dour

QATAR

Das

Sir Bu Nu'air

Sharjah

Ajman

Fujairah

Jumeriah

Dubai

Khor Kalba

Jebel Ali

Zirku

Dalma

Abu Dhabi

Bazamal Gharbi

Umm al-Nar

Sir Bani Yas

Merawah

Musaffah

KHATAM

Jebel Dhanna

Bani Yas

Al Ain

Batha

Ruwais

Buraimi
Oasis

Ghayathi

Tarif

AT TAFF

AL HUMRAH

Al Qua'a

BAYNUNAH

Tropic of Cancer

AL MUGHRIB

Meziyrah

Liwa
Oasis

OMAN

N
W   E
S

SAUDI ARABIA

cultures. Several major civilizations have had an impact on the area. Mesopotamia, the Indus Valley, Persia, Greece, and Rome all had contact with the early inhabitants of the UAE. Later, European nations such as Portugal and Great Britain left their marks. In the end, the Arabs who had settled the region and shaped its culture would gain political control.

A Time of Struggle

The destiny of the early Arab settlers was strongly influenced by geography. Vast, desert wasteland covered most of the region. Sizzling summer temperatures posed a threat to human life. Water was scarce and precious, if it could be found at all. Ninety percent of the land was unoccupied. A few settlements were located along the coasts and at desert oases. Life was so difficult that only a few people survived. No one could possibly have predicted what was about to happen.

Modern highway in the United Arab Emirates

Dramatic Change

Welcome to the modern United Arab Emirates! The lonely paths through the sand have been replaced by super-highways. Expensive cars have replaced camels as the major form of transportation. Most of the mud-brick huts and palm-frond houses are gone. Tall, shiny skyscrapers and spacious luxury villas now stand in their place. Satellite dishes, cell phones, and the Internet dominate communications. New schools, modern universities, and advanced technological colleges overflow with students.

The country has been transformed from one of the world's poorest nations into one of the wealthiest. Its oil and gas reserves are projected to last at least 150 more years. The UAE has become the most dominant trading and commercial center in the Middle East.

Since independence, the country's population has increased from 180,000 to almost 3 million. Seventy-five percent of the people are immigrants who have helped build the new nation. They have added their own special influences to the cultural landscape. Although Arabic is the official language, English is commonly used in business. Additionally, Urdu, Hindi, Farsi, Bengali, and many other languages are also spoken.

Rapid development has had its impact on the environment, however. Plants and animals that were common just a few years ago have disappeared or are in danger. Underground water resources are being used faster than nature can replace them. The government sees environmental protection as a priority.

Even with the rapid changes that have taken place, the people have not lost sight of their past. Family and religion are keys to keeping traditions intact. The country has adopted some aspects of outside culture and rejected others. In just a few short years, the UAE has captured international attention and recognition. The nation has become an outstanding citizen of the world community.

Opposite: **A busy city street scene shows the diversity of people.**

Deserts, Beaches, and Sunshine

THE UNITED ARAB EMIRATES IS A CRESCENT-SHAPED country located in the southeastern corner of the Arabian Peninsula. More than 90 percent of the nation lies less than 1,000 feet (305 meters) above sea level. With the exception of the Hajar Mountains in the north, the UAE is a remarkably flat country. It is part of the world's largest desert region. This arid area stretches across North Africa and Arabia into Iran, Pakistan, and Afghanistan. Most of the country receives less than 5 inches (13 centimeters) of rainfall per year. The winters are mild and pleasant, but the summers can be scorching with temperatures more than 122 degrees Fahrenheit (50° Celsius). The physical landscape has a fascinating set of characteristics that are waiting to be explored.

Opposite: **The Hajar Mountains near the border with Oman**

The United Arab Emirates covers approximately 32,280 square miles (83,600 square kilometers). The country is slightly larger than the Canadian province of New Brunswick and a little smaller than the U.S. state of Maine. It shares land borders with its neighbors: Qatar, Saudi Arabia, and Oman. The UAE has a lengthy coastline along the Persian (Arabian) Gulf and a short coastline on the Gulf of Oman.

An Ancient Sea

Geology has played a very important role in both the surface and the subsurface of the United Arab Emirates. Much of the land area that makes up the UAE spent millions of years under

The UAE's Geographical Features

Area: 32,280 square miles (83,600 sq km)

Highest Elevation: Jebel Yibir in the Hajar Mountains, 5,010 feet (1,527 m) above sea level

Lowest Elevation: Salamiyah, a salt flat, slightly below sea level

Longest Shared Border: With Saudi Arabia, 284 miles (457 km)

Coastline: 819 miles (1,318 km)

Largest Oasis: Liwa Oasis, a 93-mile (150-km) arc of land totally within the UAE

Annual Precipitation: Less than 5 inches (13 centimeters)

Highest Average Temperature: 120°F (49°C) in the desert in the summer

Lowest Average Temperature: 65°F (18°C) in the winter

Greatest Distance North to South: 250 miles (402 km)

Greatest Distance East to West: 350 miles (563 km)

water. During this time, thousands of feet of sediment accumulated on the sea floor. Over time, trillions of small organisms living in this sea died and settled to the bottom. Eventually, new layers of sediment formed on top of the organisms, trapping them far below the surface. Later, heat, pressure, and decomposition changed these organisms into oil and gas. When these layers of oil and gas were discovered millions of years later, it dramatically altered the way people lived in the UAE.

A Peninsula Forms

Gradually, through time, the sea receded, and the UAE emerged. It was part of a continental landmass that stretched from Africa, across Arabia, and into Asia. At that time, the Red Sea and the Persian (Arabian) Gulf didn't exist. Animals from Asia and Africa migrated freely through the region. The Arabian oryx and several species of gazelle are descendants of those African migrants. The Arabian leopard of the Hajar Mountains most likely arrived from Asia.

The Arabian Gulf

The body of water that lies between Iran and the Arabian Peninsula is a strategic geographical feature. Sixty percent of the world's oil reserves and perhaps 20 percent of its gas reserves are located in countries that border this body of water. Most world maps identify the body of water as the Persian Gulf. In the Arab world, maps refer to it as the Arabian Gulf. Seven of the eight countries that surround the gulf are Arab nations. It is a source of pride to Arabs for this body of water to be named the Arabian Gulf.

A satellite view of the Arabian Peninsula

About 25 million years ago, Earth's crust began to change, and the area now known as Arabia began to separate from what is now called Africa. Arabia was located on a plate of Earth's crust that began to drift slowly eastward, creating the Red Sea. The drifting process continues to this day. The peninsula is sliding eastward at a rate of 2 inches (5 cm) per year.

Later, as Earth's climate went through a series of changes, a depression on the eastern side of Arabia filled with water. This action created the Persian (Arabian) Gulf. Temperatures were lower and rainfall was abundant. Vast forests and grasslands covered much of Arabia, including parts of the UAE.

In the western part of the Emirate of Abu Dhabi, fossil evidence supports this dramatic climate change. It appears that a major river system existed about 6 or 7 million years ago. Subtropical savanna grasslands provided the habitat for early relatives of elephants, hippopotamuses, horses, and crocodiles.

However, the climate once again changed. The area became dry and temperatures rose. The rich ecosystems of the more humid environment collapsed and disappeared. The plants and animals that replaced them had to adapt to the hostile environment of a true desert.

Four Regions

The United Arab Emirates can be divided into four physical regions. The largest region is the desert interior, which blankets almost 70 percent of the country's land area. The second region is an area of coastal lowlands found along the shorelines of both the Persian (Arabian) Gulf and the Gulf of Oman. In the north, sharing the border with Oman, the Hajar Mountains provide a stunning change. The UAE also has more than 100 islands. These islands dot the coastal waters off the shoreline of the country.

The Desert Interior

Desert covers most of the UAE's vast interior. Beginning along the border with Qatar and Saudi Arabia, the desert stretches east to the border of Oman, and then north to the Emirate of Dubai. Only the Hajar Mountains prevent the desert from reaching the Gulf of Oman.

Sand dunes and vast open desert

Winds blow from the northwest over much of the desert region. As a result, sand dunes reach their maximum size and height in the southeastern corner of the country. Here, dunes may pile to heights of 330 feet (100 m) above the surface of the desert. The region is inhospitable and largely uninhabited.

There are two major geographical exceptions within this region. One is the Liwa Oasis, and the other is the Buraimi Oasis. At the Liwa Oasis, a series of wells pumps water from an underground aquifer. The Liwa Oasis stretches in an arc for approximately 93 miles (150 km) in the south-central part of the Emirate of Abu Dhabi. This oasis is an important producer of date palms and fodder for livestock.

The Buraimi Oasis is located at Al Ain, 80 miles (130 km) east of the capital city of Abu Dhabi. The oasis includes parts of the UAE and Oman. Water from irrigation canals (*aflaj*), springs, and underground aquifers has turned this region into a farming area. The availability of water in this harsh desert environment may have attracted the first human settlers to the Buraimi Oasis more than 5,000 years ago.

Coastal Lowlands

The coastal lowlands can be divided into two segments. The longest section of coastal lowland runs parallel to the shoreline of the Persian (Arabian) Gulf. It begins at the very northern tip of the Emirate of Ras al-Khaimah and reaches all the way to the western border with Qatar. Along the shoreline are many lagoons, estuaries, and indentations. Some of the finest mangrove forests in the country are located here. Mangroves provide important habitats for fish and birds.

On land, the coastal region is covered by fine sand and salt flats (*sabkhas*). Sabkhas are formed when high evaporation rates leave a layer of salt deposited on the surface. The white salt glimmers under the intensity of the noonday sun. It can give the illusion that the land surface is a large lake. The heavy concentration of salt creates an extremely hostile environment for plants, and only a few species of algae can survive.

Sabkhas along the Persian (Arabian) Gulf

On the southern coast, a narrow coastal plain hugs the shore of the Gulf of Oman. Coastal lagoons and marshes dot the landscape, and a rare stand of black mangroves is found at Khor Kalba in the Emirate of Sharjah. This coastline has some of the most beautiful sand beaches in the UAE.

The Hajar Mountains

The Hajar Mountains are unique in that they formed under water as an oceanic ridge. Their original materials were composed of igneous rocks, which included lava and basalt. About 15 to 20 million years ago, the portion of the ocean floor on which this material was located began to move. It was pushed into the eastern corner of the Arabian Peninsula. This shift in Earth's crust resulted in the creation of a dramatic new range of mountains.

Irrigated vegetable plots in the Hajar Mountains

The major distribution of the Hajar Mountains is in Oman. In the UAE, the range is found primarily in the Emirates of Fujairah and Ras al-Khaimah. Here, the range runs north to south for approximately 50 miles (80 km) and is generally about 20 miles (32 km) wide. The highest elevation in the UAE is Jebel Yibir, which is 5,010 feet (1,527 m) above sea level. It is located a short distance west of the town of Dibba.

Rainwater discharge from the higher elevations has carved deep cuts into both the eastern and western flanks of the mountains. These gorges, called *wadis*, are some of the few places where green vegetation can be found most of the year. The wadis have created a rugged environment, which is attracting an increasing number of tourists each year.

Offshore Islands

The islands located in the Persian (Arabian) Gulf contain approximately 2,278 square miles (5,900 sq km) of UAE territory. The most important island is Abu Dhabi. It is the site of the nation's capital, the city of Abu Dhabi. Other islands, such as Das, Zirku, Arzanah, and Al Mubarraz, are important collection points for oil and gas produced from offshore wells. The island of Sir Bani Yas has been developed into an internationally known wildlife sanctuary. The Greater and Lesser

View of the wildlife sanctuary on the island of Sir Bani Yas

Looking at Cities in the United Arab Emirates

Dubai (pictured below) is the second-largest city in the United Arab Emirates and is the capital of the Emirate of Dubai. Located on the Persian (Arabian) Gulf, the town has been involved in trade since at least 1799. In

the 1930s, Dubai was known for its pearl trade. Today, it is the country's leading center of trade and the area's chief port for importing goods from the United States and Europe. Since the late 1960s, the export of oil has made Dubai the United Arab Emirates' second-richest emirate. In recent years, tourism has become important for Dubai. Beaches, resorts, hotels, and golf courses bring many visitors. The city's old section attracts people to its outdoor markets and to buildings from the 1800s, such as the Al-Fahidi Fort and the Sheikh Saeed al-Maktoum House.

Sharjah is the third-largest city and is the capital of the Sharjah Emirate. It is located northeast of Dubai on the Persian (Arabian) Gulf. In the 1700s, Sharjah's rulers came into conflict with British interests in the

gulf. The British defeated them in 1819 and assumed military control of the region. Great Britain made Sharjah its headquarters in the gulf until 1954. Today, the city claims to be the cultural capital of the United Arab Emirates. The country's first school opened there in 1953. Today, it has archaeological, art, science, heritage, and Islamic museums. Sharjah also boasts the country's largest mosque—the King Faisal Mosque. This mosque can hold 3,000 worshipers.

Al Ain is the fourth-largest city. It is located in an oasis in eastern Abu Dhabi, near the border with Oman. Until the 1960s and 1970s, Saudi Arabia and Oman claimed parts of Al Ain. In 1966 and 1974, the border disputes were finally settled. In 1977, the United Arab Emirates' first university opened in Al Ain. Some of the country's oldest artifacts have been found near Al Ain. Today, visitors hunt for fossils on nearby Jebel Hafit. Just outside Al Ain is the Hili Archaeological Gardens with a tomb from about 3000 B.C. Hili Fun City and Ice Rink are a few miles from the gardens. There, visitors amuse themselves with more than 200 games and rides.

Ras al-Khaimah is the fifth-largest city. This ancient seaport is north of Sharjah on the Persian (Arabian) Gulf. Until 1869 and then again from 1900 to 1919, Ras al-Khaimah was part of the Sharjah Emirate. Since 1919, it has been the capital of the Ras al-Khaimah Emirate. The city of Ras al-Khaimah is in a highly agricultural area of the United Arab Emirates. Much of the city's business revolves around producing and processing dates, vegetables, and tobacco. Other industries include a lime factory and cement factories.

Tunb Islands and Abu Musa Island are currently involved in an international dispute between Iran and the UAE about ownership rights.

Solar Impact

Most of the United Arab Emirates is located between 22° and 26° north latitude. The Tropic of Cancer passes through the center of the Emirate of Abu Dhabi. The rays of the sun concentrate the maximum heat energy along the Tropic of Cancer during the summer months, which is why summers in the UAE are so hot. Summer temperatures average 93°F (34°C).

In the desert interior, temperatures may exceed 122°F (50°C) during the heat of the day. The surface temperature of the sand can approach 170°F (77°C). This is hot enough to cause serious burns to bare feet. In order to survive these temperatures, a person would have to replace 9 pints (4.26 liters) of body fluids each day. In contrast, the night temperatures can drop dramatically. Because there is seldom cloud cover and there are no large bodies of water and little vegetation, the heat energy from the sun escapes rapidly at night. The temperatures from June through September are hot across the entire country. The only exception is in the Hajar Mountains, where the higher elevation results in a slightly cooler environment.

The winter months in the UAE are from November through March and bring remarkably comfortable weather. Daily temperatures average between 77° and 95°F (25° and 35°C). The skies are mostly clear. The sun is bright, and thousands of tourists flock to the beaches.

Clear Skies

Precipitation is rare and precious in the United Arab Emirates. With few exceptions, most of the country receives less than 5 inches (13 cm) of rainfall during the year. Not only is the precipitation scarce, it is highly variable. In Dubai, the amount of rainfall in one year was 0.54 inches (1.37 cm). In a different year, Dubai recorded 8 inches (20 cm). Average rainfall numbers mean little in the UAE.

The major physical factor that creates these arid conditions across the country is the presence of a high-pressure cell. A band of high pressure, the Subtropical High Pressure Cell, straddles the UAE most of the year. In this high-pressure cell, air descends from the upper atmosphere toward Earth's surface. As the air descends, it heats and begins to evaporate moisture from the land surface. High-pressure cells bring clear skies and no condensation. As a result, the area is extremely dry.

Flash Floods

When a rare storm does bring rainfall, it can be a downpour. Much of the moisture runs off the dry, baked surface of the land. The rapid runoff can produce flash flooding. Floods may occur in the wadis on the flanks of the Hajar Mountains. Walls of water rushing through the deeply cut wadis often carry boulders the size of cars. Unsuspecting campers are sometimes surprised by the dangerous, raging torrents of fast-moving water. Sometimes these storms occur in wadis high in the mountains while, at the same time, wadis lower in the mountains are completely dry.

Drought

A deep wadi in the mountains

Even in arid environments, drought may be a serious problem. From 1999 to 2000, a dramatic decline in rainfall caused problems in the north-central and eastern regions of the UAE. The east coast averaged only about 0.25 inch (0.63 cm) of precipitation in 1999, and the year 2000 was not much better. Wells that were pumping water from underground aquifers went dry or began to produce brackish (salty) water. Crops in the area withered under the unrelenting heat of the summer sun. Villages were forced to bring in drinking water by truck. Surviving in a desert environment is not an easy task.

Survival of
the Fittest

THE UNITED ARAB EMIRATES IS A DESERT COUNTRY. Many people have the mistaken impression that arid environments will not support plant and animal life. In fact, the UAE's coastal shoreline provides a rich habitat for several species of plants and animals. The offshore islands and the waters surrounding them are teeming with life. In the mountains, rare animals fight for survival. Even in the interior, desert plant and animal species have adapted successfully to the difficult conditions in which they live.

Opposite: **Certain types of shrubs thrive in desert conditions.**

Feathered Friends

Birds can be found in every region of the UAE, even though they are scarce in the interior desert during the summer months. Records show that approximately 400 different species of birds have been seen in the UAE.

Geography plays a critical role in explaining why such a small country is so rich in bird life. The UAE is perfectly located on the major flyway between central Asia and East Africa. Each spring and fall, millions of birds make their way across Arabia. Most stop to rest and feed on their long journey between the continents. About 80 percent of birds found in the UAE are migrating from one place to another. The UAE is a convenient haven for these birds.

The Desert Squash

The desert squash is a hardy vine that grows wild and can survive in sandy desert soil with very little moisture. Many Arabs believe that eating four wild squash seeds each day will help to control particular diseases such as diabetes.

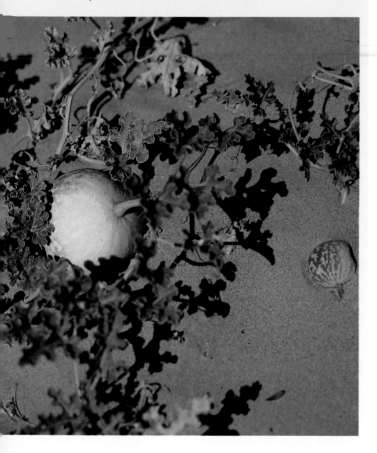

Desert Adaptation

Although the number of species of plants that live in the desert is small, several types of grasses, shrubs, and unique plants survive. These plants fall into a broad category called *xerophytes*. Xerophytes are plants that live in regions with little water. Since rain is rare in the desert, these plants have developed special techniques to conserve moisture. Some have deep roots that tap into underground water sources. Others have short reproductive cycles. After a rare rain, they quickly bloom, produce seeds, and then become dormant until the next rain. Many plants have small leaves to reduce moisture loss.

Animal species that live in the desert must also be able to survive in very high temperatures and with limited sources of water. To survive in these conditions, most desert animals are nocturnal. They only come out at night after the sun has set and the temperature begins to cool. During the day, most live in burrows to avoid the sun's intense rays. Some species spend the entire summer in their burrows in a physical state similar to hibernation. Almost all of them can survive without drinking water. Instead, they acquire the moisture they need from the foods they eat.

Lizards and Snakes

Reptiles are the most dominant animal group found in the interior desert. There are several species of lizards including geckos, spiney-tailed lizards, and monitor lizards. The monitor lizard is the most aggressive reptile in the UAE. Reaching a length of 4 feet (1.22 m), a monitor lizard eats whatever it can catch.

The spiney-tailed lizard was called a *dhab* by the original Bedouin herders who lived in the desert. Bedouin children learned to trap these lizards when the reptiles emerged from their burrows to warm their bodies in the early morning sun. The lizards were skinned and cleaned. The meat provided a tasty source of protein, and the skin was used to make leather products.

Several species of snakes live in the desert, including the sand boa, the saw-scaled viper, and the sand viper. These last two snakes are deadly. Fortunately, they try to avoid humans and are content to eat rodents, geckos, and insects.

The Little Ones

Rodents provide a food source for many of the other animals that live in the desert. They include mice, rats, jirds, gerbils, and jerboas. The jerboa is one of the most unusual rodents. It has oversized hind legs and hops about much like a kangaroo. Capable of jumping more than 6 feet (1.8 m), it uses its long tail for balance.

The Sand Boa

The sand boa is one of the desert's most interesting snakes. To escape the desert heat, it lives and travels under the sand. Its eyes and nostrils are on the top of its head. When hunting, the sand boa lies quietly beneath the sand's surface with only its eyes and nostrils slightly exposed. When a rodent or other victim approaches, the snake darts out, wraps its body around its prey, and smothers it. When the prey has ceased to struggle, the snake swallows its victim whole.

Arabian oryx in a protected area

Scarce Mammals

Many of the large mammals that once lived in the desert were hunted to extinction in the wild. The Arabian oryx disappeared in this manner, but it is currently being bred in captivity. The Arabian ostrich is gone forever. There may be a few rheem—a type of gazelle—in remote areas. A limited number of sand gazelles have been observed near the Liwa Oasis, but they too are close to extinction in the wild. Substantial numbers of Arabian red foxes and hares are still common in the desert.

Pass the Salt

The belt of coastal lowlands along the shores of the Persian (Arabian) Gulf is composed primarily of *sabkhas* (salt flats)

"The Gift of God"

The camel is the most loved and respected animal in the United Arab Emirates. Historically, the camel was critical to the survival of the early people who settled in the UAE. It was the most important means of land transport for both people and goods. The camel was also a critical source of meat and milk for food. The animal's wool was spun into yarn to make tents and rugs. The hide was converted into a bag for carrying water from oasis to oasis.

Camels are well adapted to survive in the harsh conditions of the desert. One of their greatest assets is their ability to conserve fluids. During the winter months, they can go several days without water. They are able to meet most of their water needs through the moisture found in the plants they eat. In early summer, a camel is watered every seven to nine days. Even in the hottest months, a camel can exist for two full days without drinking.

Camels have an exceptionally large water-retention capacity. They are capable of drinking up to 30 gallons (114 liters) in a few hours. They then use this water conservatively. Their body temperature can rise several

degrees without their losing valuable body moisture by sweating. The camel also possesses a unique kidney function that allows it to recycle its urine in an effort to conserve water.

Another special asset of the camel is a tough lining in its mouth that allows it to eat thorny desert plants. It has two sets of eyelashes for each eye to protect its vision from blowing sand and dust. Large padded feet allow camels to walk over loose sand without sinking into the dunes. With all of its qualities, it is no surprise that the Arabs called the camel *Ata Allah*—"The Gift of God."

and sandy plains. The sabkhas are almost completely devoid of meaningful life. Only a few species of algae can tolerate the high salt content. On the sandy plains, the salt content is still present but begins to decline. Still, it is too high for most plants. However, special plants know as *halophytes* (salt-tolerant plants) grow there. They have had to make special adaptations. For example, the tamarisk plant separates salt from the water and passes it out of its system through its leaves.

Along the Shore

The most interesting part of the coastal lowlands is the shore-line. Deep indentations created by the tides penetrate the land. These features are called creeks, or *khors*. Valuable stands of mangrove forests exist in these creeks and along coastal stretches. Mangroves are special because they actually survive and flourish in the salty seawater. They provide a critical habitat for wildlife, especially birds. They are also an important spawning and nursery site for many different species of fish and crustaceans.

The coastal lowlands along the Gulf of Oman are narrow gravel and sand plains formed by deposits from the Hajar Mountains. These alluvial deposits have been farmed for centuries. There are also beautiful sand beaches along the coast. At Khor Kalba, the largest black mangrove forest in Arabia exists. It is the home of a rare subspecies of white-collared kingfisher that is nearing extinction and must be protected.

Mountain Life

Plant life in the mountains is extremely scarce. Exposed rock and boulders cover much of the surface, and there is very little soil for plants. However, in the wadis where some soil has accumulated, lush vegetation can be found around pools of water. There are grasses, shrubs, ferns, and—at some locations—the only species of orchid that grows in the UAE. The availability of water attracted farmers to these isolated valleys to grow date palms and vegetables centuries ago. They also herded goats on the scant vegetation available at the higher slopes.

The mountains of the UAE serve as habitat for some rare animals. These animals have retreated to the most isolated part of the country in an attempt to escape contact with people. The rare Arabian tahr, a goatlike animal, is nearly extinct. The Arabian leopard is the region's most endangered animal. Only an estimated 100 of these beautiful cats still remain in the wild. The caracal lynx is also seriously threatened, but efforts are underway to prevent its extinction. A substantial increase in the number of domestic goats and donkeys is destroying much of the habitat that these animals need to survive.

A rare Arabian tahr

Endangered sand gazelles on Sir Bani Yas Island

A Marine Environment

The UAE's islands and surrounding waters are rich in biodiversity. These areas provide a significant resting and feeding ground for migratory birds. A wide variety of commercial fish supply an economic livelihood for the country's fishers. Ecologically, the islands are critical habitats for many species.

The island of Sir Bani Yas has been converted into a private nature reserve. Thousands of trees provide commercial fruit and habitat for wildlife. Herds of endangered sand gazelles, Arabian gazelles,

Green Turtles

Green turtles are one of seven species of endangered marine turtles that are found in the oceans. They nest on both coasts of the UAE, on the shores of several islands, and in protected areas in the neighboring Sultanate of Oman. The turtles return to lay their eggs on the same beach where they were hatched.

In preparation for laying her eggs, the female green turtle scoops out a hole in the sand with her front flippers. Then she lays an average of 110 golf ball–sized eggs and covers them with sand. The mother returns to the ocean with little chance of ever seeing her offspring. The eggs hatch in about eight weeks. Only 2 or 3 out of every 10,000 hatchlings will survive to maturity. As a result, the numbers of green turtles are steadily declining.

Arabian oryx, and scimitar-horned oryx are bred in captivity on the island. It is hoped that they can eventually be released into the wild to populate the country's deserts once again.

The shallow sea around the islands of Merawah, Butinah, and Bazam al-Gharbi are being considered as possible sites for a marine reserve. These shallow waters support an extensive area of sea-grass beds. The sea grasses are essential for the survival of the rare dugongs (sea cows) and a feeding population of endangered green turtles.

Protecting the Innocent

Many animals and plants in the United Arab Emirates have become extinct. Other species are endangered or seriously threatened. Numerous factors have contributed to this situation. The government and the private sector are working hard to solve the problem.

In the past, many animals were hunted to extinction or near extinction to provide food for families. Others were killed because they were predators that ate domestic animals such as goats. To halt this process, Sheikh Zayed banned hunting in Abu Dhabi more than twenty years ago. In 1983, the government made it illegal to shoot birds or to hunt gazelles and hares anywhere in the UAE. Today, hunting with guns is banned throughout the country.

Loss of habitat has been the most serious problem for many animals. Overgrazing by camels and goats is destroying vegetation. The expansion of cities, the building of roads, and the work of oil- and gas-exploration crews are unintentionally harming critical habitats. To help balance the negative impact, several important programs have been initiated. In 1992, the government established the Federal Environmental Agency. The agency's task is to reduce marine pollution, control air emissions, halt water and soil contamination, protect groundwater resources, and create public awareness regarding environmental problems.

In other governmental action, the UAE became the first country to prohibit fishers from bottom-trawling in its waters. The Ministry of Agriculture and Fisheries also issued a significant decree. That decree forbids catching sea turtles or collecting their eggs.

In private action, Sheikh Sultan bin Muhammad al-Qassimi, ruler of the Emirate of Sharjah, established the Arabian Leopard Trust. He donated a large land area in the Hajar Mountains for a protected reserve. The trust hopes to breed the rare Arabian leopard and caracal lynx in captivity and return them to the protected area. In the Emirate of Dubai, Crown Prince Sheikh Muhammad bin Rashid al-Maktoum created the nation's first wildlife sanctuary. The 124-acre (50-hectare) plot of tidal mudflats provides protection for migratory birds.

Few nations have moved more quickly to protect their environment. Much of this action is the result of the leadership of the president, Sheikh Zayed bin Sultan al-Nahyan. In recognition of that leadership and citizen participation, the UAE was awarded the 1997 Golden Panda Award from the World Wide Fund for Nature.

The Impact
of Humans

Establishing the early historical records of the United Arab Emirates has not been an easy task. Prior to independence in 1971, very little archaeological investigation had taken place. The first professional archaeological site was at Umm al-Nar in 1958. Since then, several other sites have been excavated and many new sites have been discovered. In the future, these sites may yield a clearer understanding of the country's earliest residents.

The first documented evidence of humans in the UAE was discovered in the foothills of the Hajar Mountains. People were most likely present at these locations between 6000 and 5000 B.C. The sites have revealed some excellent flint arrowheads, blades, knives, and drills.

In 1959, Danish archaeologists uncovered tombs at Jebel Hafit and Jebel al-Emalah estimated to date from about 3000 B.C. Some of the tombs had pottery fragments from objects that had been imported from Mesopotamia. This evidence suggests that these early inhabitants traded with other groups some distance away.

Opposite: **Remains of ancient pottery found near Al Ain**

The Great Hili Tomb dates back to the third century B.C.

Umm al-Nar

Between 2500 and 2000 B.C., the Umm al-Nar culture developed. During this time, fishing and farming villages were established at several different sites. Each village featured a fortress tower that was 52–82 feet (16–25 m) in diameter. In the center of each fort was the most precious treasure—a water well. This water source was essential to the success of the farming community. The people irrigated the land to grow date palms, cereals, fruits, and vegetables.

The Umm al-Nar culture also left behind a rich legacy in their tombs. The tombs reveal superb masonry work, some with carvings of camels and gazelles. Most of the tombs of this period were circular.

They had a diameter of 13–46 feet (4–14 m). The larger tombs served as the burial sites for hundreds of individuals.

Analysis of the skeletal remains from these tombs indicates interesting medical problems. For example, the bones show evidence of staph and strep infections as well as lesions and arthritis. However, the most dramatic discovery came from a tomb near Tell Abraq. Doctors examined the skeleton of a young woman who died when she was about twenty years old. The examination showed that she suffered from polio. This skeleton is the earliest evidence of polio anywhere in the world.

Two significant events occurred in the UAE during the period from 1200 to 300 B.C. The first was the domestication of the camel, which revolutionized transportation in the desert and opened new trade opportunities. The second was the development of *falaj* irrigation, which used underground channels to bring water from the mountains to the desert. Some ancient falaj are still in use in the Al Ain area.

In the latter part of the first millennium B.C., Mleiha, a prosperous camel caravan town, flourished in the interior of the Emirate of Sharjah. This town was a large settlement covering several square miles. Artifacts found during excavation show that the people traded with others in what are now the nations of Iran, Iraq, Saudi Arabia, Bahrain, and Greece.

Between A.D. 1 and A.D. 200, Ad Dour, the most powerful and important coastal city in the gulf, prospered. Ad Dour's merchants were known far and wide. The Ad Dour ruins are situated along a coastal lagoon in the Emirate of Umm al-Qaiwain. The ancient city had an early religious significance. Belgian archaeologists uncovered the remains of a temple site that was dedicated to a sun deity named Shams.

Between 200 and 600, Arab migrations continued to flow into what are today's emirates. Some of these people came from Yemen, and others arrived from Saudi Arabia. They engaged in various activities including fishing, caravan trade, farming, and nomadic grazing. The tribes governed themselves through a time-honored system of consultation and consensus known as "desert democracy."

Islam Arrives

The year A.D. 610 marked an important event. It was the beginning of Islam in Mecca, Saudi Arabia, under the leadership of the Prophet Muhammad. Islam emphasized a return to the teachings of the Prophet Abraham. Like Judaism and Christianity, the religion was monotheistic—its followers believed in one God. Islam, which means "submission," stresses that people should yield to the will of God.

In 630, the Prophet Muhammad sent a missionary from Mecca to southeastern Arabia. The missionary invited the people to convert to Islam. The most powerful tribe in southeastern Arabia, the Azd, accepted the invitation. The Azd also invited others throughout the region to convert. When the Prophet Muhammad died two years later, wars broke out in protest against Islamic rule in much of Arabia. To put down the revolt, a Muslim army marched to Dibba, along the Gulf of Oman. In the hard-fought battle that followed, the Muslim forces defeated their enemies. Today, on the plains behind Dibba, countless grave markers pay homage to those who perished in the fight.

Over the next few centuries, the inhabitants of today's UAE followed their daily routines. Life had few changes as the residents of the interior desert struggled to maintain the most basic existence. Along the coast, fishing, pearling, and trade were carried out.

It was during this period that the great merchant city of Julfar, in Ras al-Khaimah, dominated the lower gulf. The city's sailors were great navigators who sailed throughout the gulf to the Indian Ocean and around Arabia to East Africa's ports. In their seaworthy *dhows* they also sailed to southern India, Sri Lanka, Vietnam, and China. Pieces of fine Vietnamese and Chinese pottery have recently been recovered from ruins at Julfar.

Unwanted Visitors

Portugal, a great seafaring nation, sent Vasco da Gama around the Cape of Good Hope in Africa. Vasco da Gama's journey introduced Europe to the rich trading opportunities in the gulf. The Portuguese recognized quickly that in order to benefit from the profitable trade in the Persian (Arabian) Gulf, they would have to control the Strait of Hormuz. In 1507, Portuguese nobleman and adventurer Alfonso de Albuquerque captured the fortress on the island of Hormuz, which guarded the entrance to the gulf.

Ahmed bin Majid

Ahmed bin Majid was a great scholar-navigator. He was born in Julfar in the early 1430s. After memorizing the Holy Qur'an (Islam's holy book) at an early age, he studied geography, astronomy, and literature.

In 1489, he completed his most famous work, *The Benefits and Principles of Oceanography*. The book included information on the history of navigation, compasses, naval routes, astronomy, meteorology, ocean currents, and wind patterns. In 1498, Ahmed bin Majid assisted the famous Portuguese explorer Vasco da Gama in his voyage around the Cape of Good Hope to India. Today, his written works are still studied by scholars.

For more than a century, the Portuguese controlled gulf shipping. They built forts in Mattrah and Muscat, Oman, as well as in Manama on the island of Bahrain. They also established a tax collection house in Julfar. The Portuguese imposed heavy taxes and, in general, treated the people of the region badly. Those who opposed the Portuguese were imprisoned. Prisoners received harsh treatment and occasionally had their ears and noses cut off to "set an example."

A Portuguese fort on the gulf

Portuguese control of the Perisan (Arabian) Gulf region was soon challenged by other European powers, including the British and the Dutch. Great Britain established a foothold in India in 1600. India proved to be a profitable colony for the British. Portuguese interference with their trade from India was a major annoyance. In 1622, the British navy, with the assistance of Persian ground troops, captured Hormuz. This signaled the end of Portuguese control in the gulf. The British became the dominant foreign power in the region.

At first, the British paid little attention to developments in the emirates. Their primary interest was focused on keeping gulf shipping lanes open. On land, political control passed first to powerful tribes in Oman. Later, for a brief period, the region fell under Persian influence. However, by the mid-eighteenth century, two powerful tribes from within the territory began to exert their influence in the region. One tribe was the Qawasim. They established a strong maritime presence in the coastal region of the northern emirates. Qawasim descendants currently rule Ras al-Khaimah and Sharjah.

The second tribe was the Bani Yas. In the interior, the Bani Yas established widespread control from their base at the Liwa Oasis. In 1761, a Bani Yas hunting expedition tracked a gazelle from the coastal desert onto Abu Dhabi Island. Here, they discovered a large freshwater well. The Al-Nahyans were the ruling tribe of the Bani Yas. They moved to Abu Dhabi in 1793 and constructed a fort over the well.

In 1833, the Emirate of Dubai was established by the Al-Bu Falasah tribe, which was a branch of the Bani Yas. The Al-Maktoum family, who currently rule Dubai, are the leading family of the Al-Bu Falasah. During the twentieth century, the Al-Nahyans and the Al-Maktoums would emerge as the most powerful political families in the UAE.

A Qawasim Challenge

The British had little to do with the Bani Yas since they did not challenge British maritime supremacy in the gulf. The Qawasim, on the other hand, had a powerful naval presence in the region. At the end of the eighteenth century, the Qawasim had 20,000 sailors and a fleet of more than sixty large wooden dhows. Their main rival for regional maritime control was the Al-Bu Said family in Oman.

In 1798, the Al-Bu Saids signed a treaty with the British. In the eyes of the Qawasim, anyone who was an ally of a rival was also a rival. Since the British were now considered enemies, their trading vessels became fair targets for Qawasim raids. The British considered these attacks as acts of piracy and labeled the lower gulf the "Pirate Coast." Local UAE historians argued that the British were the outsiders, and the Qawasim were merely protecting their sphere of influence.

The British decided to put an end to Qawasim interference in the gulf. They launched a major naval attack from Bombay, India, in 1819. After capturing or burning every Qawasim boat they could find, the British Royal Navy occupied

Falaya Fort, where the 1820 treaty was signed

the Qawasim forts at Ras al-Khaimah. In 1820, they forced a General Treaty of Peace on all of the sheikhdoms of the lower gulf. Other treaties aimed at preserving peace in the region followed in 1835 and 1853. Finally, in 1892, the British cemented their control over the gulf sheikdoms. The sheikhs signed a series of agreements with the British to accept formal British protection. In return, the sheikhs agreed to have no dealings with any foreign power without the permission of the British.

The Evolution of Leadership

Having secured political and military control of the region, the British paid little attention to domestic development within the emirates. They were pretty much free to conduct business as usual, as long as it wasn't with a foreign power. For an extended period, Sharjah was the dominant emirate. Then Abu Dhabi, under the charismatic leadership of Sheikh Zayed bin Mohammed (Zayed the Great), assumed prominence. His rule lasted from 1855 until 1909. When he died, a family squabble over who would become the next leader weakened Abu Dhabi's leadership position.

With somewhat of a political power void in the emirates, the leadership of the Emirate of Dubai stepped forward. The Al-Maktoum family began to encourage trade. They supported the development of a major port on the creek in Dubai. It would be difficult to overemphasize the positive impact that Sheikh Rashid bin Saeed al-Maktoum had on the Emirate of Dubai. He is sometimes affectionately referred to as the "Father of Dubai."

Sheikh Rashid first served as regent to his ruling father, Sheikh Saeed, because of his father's illness. When his father died in 1958, he became the ruler of Dubai. Since he had nearly twenty years of experience as second-in-command, the transition to power was very smooth. He would serve as the ruler of Dubai until 1990. During this period, he used his considerable political skills to turn Dubai into the most important commercial and trade center in the gulf.

During the same period, Sheikh Shakhbut of the Al-Nahyan family had assumed power in Abu Dhabi. His job was difficult. Economic hard times had fallen on the emirate as a result of the collapse of the pearling industry. He was desperate for an opportunity to end the conditions of poverty for his people. In 1939, Sheikh Shakhbut allowed a British company to drill for oil. Later, in 1953, he allowed an Anglo-French company to drill for oil offshore. Six years later, the Anglo-French company discovered a major reserve of oil under the coastal waters of Abu Dhabi.

Offshore oil drilling rig in the port of Abu Dhabi

Oil and Politics

Petroleum was first exported in 1962, and the oil era began. Geologists were quick to discover that Abu Dhabi had enormous reserves of oil and gas. Once Abu Dhabi began to export oil, money flowed into the treasury. Managing this new wealth was a difficult task for Sheikh Shakhbut because he did not trust banks and he was suspicious of the foreign oil companies. Eventually, the ruling Al-Nahyan family encouraged him to step aside in favor of his brother. In 1966, Sheikh Zayed bin Sultan al-Nahyan was selected as the ruler of Abu Dhabi.

Sheikh Zayed had a strong record of excellent leadership as ruler's representative in the oasis village of Al Ain. He served in this position from 1946 until his selection as ruler of Abu Dhabi two decades later. He had a reputation for making good decisions. Moving quickly as the new ruler, he used the oil wealth to transform Abu Dhabi into a progressive, modern society. He also shared Abu Dhabi's wealth with those emirates that were not blessed with significant oil reserves.

In 1968, two years after Sheikh Zayed had assumed power in Abu Dhabi, the British made a startling announcement. They stated that they were terminating all their defense agreements east of Suez. After almost four centuries, the British planned to end their dominance in the Persian (Arabian) Gulf.

Birth of a Nation

The British suggested a federation for the gulf sheikhdoms of Bahrain, Qatar, Abu Dhabi, Dubai, Sharjah, Ras al-Khaimah,

Fujairah, Umm al-Qaiwain, and Ajman. The British were determined to leave by the end of 1971. A political marriage of emirates with different economic bases and divergent political views would not be easy to arrange. As the deadline for unification approached, numerous problems could not be solved. Bahrain and Qatar ultimately opted to establish independent countries. Six of the other seven sheikhdoms agreed to form the United Arab Emirates in 1971. Finally, in 1972, the last holdout, the Emirate of Ras al-Khaimah, joined the federation.

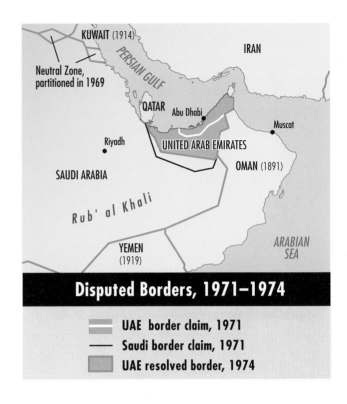

Disputed Borders, 1971–1974

UAE border claim, 1971
Saudi border claim, 1971
UAE resolved border, 1974

The new country was formally recognized as an independent nation on December 2, 1971. Few foreign critics believed the federation would succeed. However, under the extraordinary leadership of Sheikh Zayed, Sheikh Rashid, and the other rulers, the UAE has become a model of Arab unity.

A student sign celebrates the National Day of Independence.

Establishing a Federation

THE CITIZENS OF THE UNITED ARAB EMIRATES ARE participants in a unique political experience. The act of merging individual emirates into a single political unit was a complex process. Difficult decisions had to be made regarding how much authority would be given to the federal government. At times, the question of how much power would remain with the individual emirates exceeded all other considerations. Moreover, the leaders of the new country had no choice but to protect and practice the time-honored tradition of consultation and consensus.

The United Arab Emirates (*Dawlat al-Imarat al-Arabiyya al-Muttahida* in Arabic) was recognized as an independent

Opposite: **Business area of Abu Dhabi**

The Majlis

The *majlis*, or council, has been the heart of traditional government in the emirates for centuries. The practice still continues today, with each of the emirate rulers and other respected family leaders holding open meetings. All citizens are welcome to attend. The reasons for attendance differ substantially. One person may come to request a scholarship for a child to study overseas. Another may request land for a farm. Sometimes groups petition the leader regarding their concern about business; economic and social issues, such as the high cost of marriage; or increasing salt content in their water wells.

Sheikh Zayed frequently travels throughout the country to provide his citizens personal access to their leader. The ruler of the Emirate of Fujairah holds an open majlis every week. During the holy month of Ramadan, he holds daily meetings. Through this technique, rulers and chiefs retain the loyalty and support of their people. Without that support, their authority would not survive. Every citizen has the opportunity to be directly involved in government decision making. That is why the majlis system has often been referred to as "desert democracy."

Abu Dhabi: Did You Know This?

Location: On Abu Dhabi Island in the Persian (Arabian) Gulf

Altitude: 16 feet (5 m) above sea level

Population: 500,000 (1990 est.)

Year founded: 1761

Founders: Tribespeople of the Bani Yas

Average temperatures: January, 64°F (18°C); July, 91°F (33°C)

Average annual precipitation: 4.1 inches (10.5 cm)

Abu Dhabi, the capital of the Emirate of Abu Dhabi, is also the capital of the United Arab Emirates. The city is located on the southeast shore of the Persian (Arabian) Gulf. Until the 1960s, Abu Dhabi was a fishing village. Oil was discovered in the desert in 1960, and production began two years later. The high income from oil production has changed the village into a modern city of high-rise buildings, with an international airport. The national library is located in Abu Dhabi.

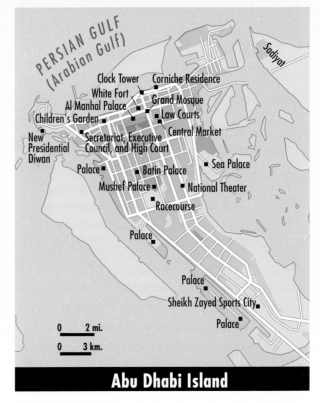

PERSIAN GULF (Arabian Gulf)

Sadiyat

Clock Tower
Corniche Residence
White Fort
Al Manhal Palace
Grand Mosque
Children's Garden
Law Courts
Central Market
New Presidential Diwan
Secretariat, Executive Council, and High Court
Palace
Batin Palace
Sea Palace
Mushef Palace
National Theater
Racecourse
Palace
Palace
Sheikh Zayed Sports City
Palace

0   2 mi.
0   3 km.

Abu Dhabi Island

nation on December 2, 1971. A provisional Constitution was adopted in July 1971. It contained 151 articles outlining the political evolution of the new state. This Constitution was made permanent in 1996.

NATIONAL GOVERNMENT OF THE UNITED ARAB EMIRATES

Executive Branch

SUPREME COUNCIL OF RULERS

PRESIDENT

PRIME MINISTER

VICE PRESIDENT

FEDERAL COUNCIL OF MINISTERS

Legislative Branch

SUPREME COUNCIL OF RULERS

COUNCIL OF MINISTERS

FEDERAL NATIONAL COUNCIL

Judicial Branch

SUPREME COURT

COURTS OF FIRST INSTANCE

Supreme Council of Rulers

The highest political authority in the federal government is the Supreme Council of Rulers. The council is composed of the seven rulers of the individual emirates, who exercise both executive and legislative powers. They elect the UAE president and vice president from their council of seven. Council members are also charged with ratifying federal laws and international treaties and preparing a federal budget. Each ruler has a single vote. However, the rulers of Abu Dhabi and Dubai have the power to veto important resolutions.

President and Vice President

Both the president and the vice president serve five-year terms and may be reelected. In fact, Sheikh Zayed has been elected to five consecutive terms as president. He has been the only president of the UAE since independence. The president presides over Supreme Council meetings and is responsible for representing the UAE when dealing with foreign leaders and governments. He requests the Supreme Council's approval of his choice for prime minister. If approved, the president and the prime minister form the cabinet, or Council of Ministers.

Council of Ministers

The Council of Ministers is composed of twenty-one members. In the past, they have been the major source of legislative proposals. They also assist in preparing the federal budget and supervise the implementation of federal laws and Supreme Court actions.

Federal National Council

The Federal National Council (FNC) is made up of forty members. The number of members that represent each emirate varies with the size of the emirate, its population, and its resources. Abu Dhabi and Dubai, which are the two largest emirates in size

Sheikh Zayed bin Sultan al-Nahyan

Sheikh Zayed is considered by many people to be the elder statesman in the Arab world. He has won the respect and admiration of leaders from across the globe. He has also earned the respect and deep affection of the citizens of the United Arab Emirates.

Sheikh Zayed began his government service in Al Ain in 1946 as the ruler's representative of Abu Dhabi's eastern region. Early in his career, he established a reputation for wisdom and fairness. Most significantly, he applied the principles of "desert democracy" through consultation and consensus before making decisions. He modernized irrigation and water rights at the Buraimi Oasis in Al Ain and strengthened its economic base.

In 1966, the Al-Nahyan family asked him to become the ruler of the Emirate of Abu Dhabi. Sheikh Zayed has retained that position ever since. His biggest task has been to manage the emirate's oil revenues

wisely for the benefit of its citizens. As ruler, he has helped guide the emirate from a poorly developed economy to a prosperous society.

In 1968, when the British announced their withdrawal from the gulf, Sheikh Zayed led the movement for federation of the seven gulf sheikhdoms. His willingness to share Abu Dhabi's oil wealth to develop the federation was an important factor in the formation of the UAE. His quiet leadership in obtaining consensus through consultation with the other emirate rulers was also significant.

When the United Arab Emirates became an independent nation on December 2, 1971, the other rulers elected Sheikh Zayed as president. Since then, he has led the UAE with patience, intelligence, fairness, and compassion. Few leaders have placed their personal imprint on the soul of a nation as significantly as Sheikh Zayed has.

and population, each have eight members. Six members represent Sharjah and Ras al-Khaimah. Fujairah, Umm al-Qaiwain, and Ajman each have four representatives. The rulers of each emirate select their representatives for the FNC.

The FNC can summon ministers to its chambers to review and analyze the work of a particular ministry. This occurs on occasions when council members receive complaints from citizens in their emirate. They also review each proposed law and express their support or disapproval of the recommended legislation. However, their role is strictly advisory, and the Supreme Council makes the final decision.

The Judicial System

The Constitution requires that the federal judicial system be an independent branch of the government. The highest court in the land is the Supreme Court. It consists of five judges who are appointed by the Supreme Council of Rulers. These judges rule on the constitutionality of federal laws and hear legal cases involving disputes between emirates. They are also the final court of appeal for cases from lower courts.

The Courts of First Instance are primarily involved in commercial and civil cases between the federal government and private citizens. They also preside over civil and criminal violations within the national capital.

A system of courts also exists in each emirate. These courts try cases that do not fall under federal jurisdiction. All of the emirates have civil courts as well as *shari'a* courts. The shari'a courts apply Islamic law, which is derived from the Holy Qur'an.

Division of Responsibilities

For the federation to be successful, all of the emirates had to give up some independence and decision making to the federal government. These issues were resolved by lengthy consultations until consensus was reached. Among the most important constitutional responsibilities granted to the federal authorities were foreign affairs, security and defense, education, public health, communications, immigration, and labor relations.

The Constitution reserved for the individual emirates powers not assigned to the federal government. The emirates' responsibilities include water issues, electricity, public works, and most important, the control of commerce. The trade issue was especially important to Dubai, which had become the commercial center of the gulf.

Municipality building in Dubai

Political power continues to filter down from the emirate to the municipalities. All of the major cities have large buildings that house the offices of the local city governments. Zoning issues, building permits, construction restrictions, and other typical city services are the responsibility of the municipal governments.

In small villages, particularly in remote regions, a local representative is the major authority. The ruler of the emirate selects him because of his high standing in the community. His fellow tribesmen have confidence and respect in his leadership. They express their concerns to him, and those that require the attention of higher authorities are passed on to emirate leaders. It is a combination of the traditional system with the new structure of government.

International Relations

The United Arab Emirates rapidly earned the respect of the international community. The country has been an outspoken supporter of the Middle East peace process and Palestinian rights. Sheikh Zayed and the UAE were one of the first nations to offer support to Kuwait after the Iraqi invasion. The UAE committed troops to the United Nations' forces to restore peace to war-weary Somalia. When Bosnia's Muslim community was under genocidal attack from the Serbs, Sheikh Zayed made an impassioned plea for the international community to respond. The nation has been one of the most generous countries in the world. More than U.S.$5 billion in aid has been allocated to more than forty developing countries.

While the UAE has been a generous and compassionate world citizen, it has also been the victim of an international injustice. When the British withdrew their military protection from the emirates in 1971, Iran quickly seized three islands claimed by the UAE. The islands were Greater Tunb, Lesser Tunb, and Abu Musa. In the hope of a peaceful solution, the

UAE requested that Iran agree to diplomatic efforts to solve the problem. Iranian diplomats have met with UAE officials from time to time to discuss improving relations. However, Iran has refused to consider returning the islands to the UAE. They also refuse to remove military bases established on the islands. The UAE also suggested that the International Court of Justice could resolve the issue. Iran has refused to participate.

Its strategic geographical location and rich oil and gas reserves require the UAE to maintain a modern military force. Over the past few years, the country has spent between 4 and 6 percent of its annual income for defense purposes. In 1999, the army had 59,000 troops. The air force was composed of 4,000 airmen, and the navy had 1,500 sailors. One of the nation's proudest achievements is the recent creation of a women's corps in the armed forces.

The National Flag

The national flag of the United Arab Emirates was officially adopted on December 2, 1971. It is rectangular in shape with its length doubling its width. There are four different-colored stripes. Nearest the mast is a vertical red stripe that covers one-quarter the length of the flag. To the right of the red vertical stripe are three equal-sized horizontal stripes. The top stripe is green, the middle is white, and the bottom stripe is black. The red, green, white, and black colors were taken from the Arab Revolt flag of 1917. These colors were included in a thirteenth-century poem. The poem relates the green Arab lands defended in black battles by blood-red swords of Arabs whose deeds are pure white.

Black Gold

A HALF-CENTURY AGO, THE FIRST OIL-DRILLING RIG punched a hole in the desert sands of the United Arab Emirates. Little more than dust came out of that hole, but the search continued. In 1950, what is now the UAE was one of the least-developed areas in the world. There were no paved roads, no schools, no hospitals, no factories, and few opportunities. The estimated 150,000 people who lived there had one of the lowest standards of living among the world's developing regions. Now, the country is one of the most modern and prosperous countries in the world. The pace of that change is nothing short of an economic miracle.

Opposite: **Oil refinery tanks near Abu Dhabi**

In the Beginning

For many centuries, the people who lived in the UAE struggled to eke out a mere existence. They engaged in either nomadic grazing, fishing, pearling, or subsistence farming near isolated oases. The desert environment made survival difficult, and the land could support only a few people.

The people were members of various tribal groups. As a group they were referred to as *Bedouin* or *Bedu*. Some lived at oases where water was available. When the winter rains came, they would move their herds of camels, goats, and sheep across the desert in search of new vegetation.

Black Gold **61**

Women usually stayed at the oases to tend the date palms and gardens. On occasion, they traveled with the men. In the desert camps, the role of each individual was well established. Daily life was guided by age and gender. Males were the dominant gender at all age levels. However, women usually held the upper hand in administering the family's domestic affairs. Respect for elders was a tradition of Arab society, and that tradition continues today. Children were seen and not heard. In the evenings, they frequently gathered at the feet of their elders to listen to stories and poems. The Bedouin were great poets and storytellers.

In the heat of the summer, when vegetation was scarce, the Bedouin returned to the oases. Dates were the staple in the Bedouin diet, and they were eaten daily. Dates have a very high caloric content and are an excellent source of energy. The date palm tree had other uses. The frond, or woody shaft of the leaf, was used to construct shelters called *barasti*. Along the coast, this woody shaft was also used to make small boats known as *shasha*. The softer tissue of the leaf was used to weave fans, baskets, and food covers. Fibers of the tree's bark were woven into rope. The date palm was an essential part of Bedouin life.

The coastal residents also had date palm groves. However, most of their attention was focused on the sea. Fishing was the major activity for most of the year. Their diets consisted largely of fish and rice. The month of June brought a drastic change in their routine when the pearling season arrived.

Baskets and other items
made from date palm fronds

Diving for Treasure

Archaeological evidence of pearling in the Persian (Arabian) Gulf can be traced to about 3000 B.C. Pearls from the UAE were traded in Baghdad in the eighth and ninth centuries A.D. By the end of the nineteenth century, pearls were in peak demand. During these years, pearl sales accounted for nearly 90 percent of the income generated in the UAE.

Generally, the pearling boats left their ports in early June and returned in late September. The boats had a crew of eighteen to

This fountain in an Abu Dhabi park honors the pearl industry.

twenty members, plus a captain. The oyster banks were several miles out into the gulf's waters. The captain decided where to anchor the boat and how long to stay in one spot.

The divers entered the water about an hour after dawn and continued to dive until sunset. During the day, they took short breaks for prayers, and a little time for coffee and dates. The crews worked in two-man teams. The diver descended with a wire basket attached to a rope. He also had a stone weight attached to his ankle to help him reach the bottom quickly. Good divers dived to depths of 100 feet (30 m). They stayed on the bottom for up to two minutes. After the diver had filled his basket with oysters, or had run out of air, he tugged on his rope. On deck, his partner quickly pulled him to the surface and emptied the basket. A short time later, the diver once again plunged to the bottom of the sea.

Pearling was a dangerous occupation, but a necessary job for the diver to support his family. Sharks could sever a limb, stonefish could inject deadly poison, and jellyfish tentacles could burn skin. Although it was a difficult profession, the discovery of a large pearl brought great joy to the entire crew.

During the 1920s, the Japanese developed a technique for making cultured pearls on a mass-production basis. They flooded the market with lower-cost pearls. At about the same time, an economic depression hit Europe and the United States, the major markets for UAE pearls. Suddenly, the natural pearl market collapsed. Hard times fell on the country, and the people suffered a devastating blow to their major source of income. The future looked bleak and forbidding.

Flames flare from an oil well.

A New Economy

In 1937, Sheikh Saeed, the ruler of Dubai, opened the emirates to oil exploration. Sheikh Shakhbut of Abu Dhabi followed by granting an onshore concession in 1939 and on offshore concession in 1953. In 1959, the first big oil reserve was discovered in the gulf, off the coast of Abu Dhabi. One year later, huge reserves in Abu Dhabi's desert were discovered. In 1966, Dubai struck a large pool of oil below the gulf's waters and Sharjah and Ras al-Khaimah followed with modest discoveries of oil.

The United Arab Emirates is a leading member of the Organization of Petroleum Exporting Countries (OPEC), established in 1960. OPEC creates a quota system for each member based on the size of the country's reserves. By controlling the production of its members, OPEC attempts to keep the price of oil profitable for the benefit of its members. In theory, that concept should be successful. However, some members violate their

A Top Ranking

The United Arab Emirates ranks third in the world in proven oil reserves, with 98.1 billion barrels. The Emirate of Abu Dhabi has more than 90 percent of the country's reserves, with 92 billion barrels. Dubai has 4.6 billion barrels, and Sharjah and Ras al-Khaimah control the remaining reserves. At current production rates, the nation's oil should last for at least 150 years.

quota restrictions and produce too much oil. When this happens, oil prices drop and become unstable. If an oil-producing country depends too heavily on oil for income, price fluctuations can damage its economy. As a result, the political leadership of the UAE has been rapidly diversifying its economy. It does not want to depend solely on oil.

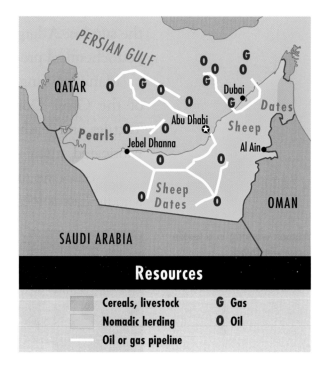

The UAE is also a world leader in natural gas reserves, with more than 200 trillion cubic feet (5.66 trillion cubic meters) of gas. The country ranks fourth in the world after Russia, Iran, and Qatar. At current production rates, the natural gas reserves should last about 200 years.

Natural gas has been a critical resource for the UAE as it has developed its economic infrastructure. Gas is used to generate electricity and to desalinate seawater. It is also injected into oil basins to improve the recovery rate of oil. Some gas is exported to Japan, Korea, and Taiwan. In the future, India and Pakistan may become major customers.

A cargo ship at the port of Jebel Ali

With the port in place, construction on the warehouses and manufacturing plants began. To attract investors, the Jebel Ali Free Zone offered attractive benefits. Any business that chose to come to the free zone could have 100 percent foreign ownership. There would be no corporate taxes and no personal income taxes. A supply of well-trained labor was guaranteed. A modern infrastructure with good roads, communications, and electricity would be provided.

Today, more than 1,500 companies from eighty-eight countries are located in the Jebel Ali Free Zone. Sharjah, Fujairah, and Umm al-Qaiwain followed with their own free zones. Soon Abu Dhabi will complete the Sadiyat Free Zone just 3.5 miles (6 km) from Abu Dhabi City. This free zone will specialize in bulk-commodity trading. Precious metals, gems, oil, grains, and ore will be among the products traded. Sadiyat Free Zone is expected to generate U.S.$7 billion in profits in the next twenty-five years.

Technology

In 2000, the UAE established Internet City, a free-trade zone for business done over the Internet. Internet City is in Dubai. Also located in Dubai is Media City, a hub for global media companies established in 2001.

Turning the Desert Green

Thirty years ago, Sheikh Zayed raised international eyebrows when he stated, "We will turn the desert green!" Always a

Irrigation allows farming in the desert.

Halophytes

One hope for the future is the development of halophytes—salt-tolerant plants that can be used for livestock and human consumption. The UAE has been a world leader in this field. The Sheikh Zayed Center for Salt Tolerant Plants near Al Ain has conducted research for several years. In 1999, a new Biosaline Agriculture Center opened for research near Dubai. The UAE donated 247 acres (100 ha) of land, and the Islamic Development Bank provided U.S.$22 million for construction and operation. The international community will be watching closely as the center develops plants that can be irrigated with varying levels of saline water.

man of his word, Sheikh Zayed has followed through on his promise. Today, more than 150 million trees hold back the desert dunes and line the superhighways that cross the country. An additional 25 million date palms have been planted. Many of them were created at a palm-tissue culture center. At the center, tissue is removed from a live palm tree and incubated in a test tube to produce a new tree. Parks and gardens have converted the major cities from barren sand flats into havens of lush vegetation. To maintain these beautiful trees and flowers, the cities use recycled wastewater to conserve scant supplies of freshwater.

In the past ten years, the acreage of cultivated land has increased more than 100 percent. The UAE is self-sufficient in animal fodder and date production and meets two-thirds of its vegetable needs. Dairy farms produce almost all of the domestic milk consumption. Poultry farms and sheep, goat, and camel producers have also seen substantial increases in production.

The government provides farmers with free land, machinery, and seeds. It drills wells in rural areas. It also constructs dams in the mountains to catch and retain precipitation runoff. The Ministry of Agriculture provides assistance in the use of pesticides and fertilizers.

The major problem facing agriculture is the availability and quality of water. The rapid increase in water use is threatening underground aquifers. Some wells have gone dry, while others have been invaded by brackish water. Drip irrigation techniques and other water conservation methods are being emphasized.

System of Weights and Measures

The United Arab Emirates uses the metric system. The British imperial gallon and U.S. measurements are also used. For example, 5 imperial gallons equals 6 U.S. gallons or 23 liters.

Foreign Visitors

Tourism has become a steadily increasing source of revenue for the UAE. The Emirates of Dubai, Ras al-Khaimah, Sharjah, and Fujairah have all invested heavily in an attempt to attract tourists. Mild, sunny winters, an almost total absence of crime, and stunning five-star hotels are a major attraction. In addition, water parks, golf courses, racetracks, bird watching, and shopping in the tax-free zones all contribute to the lure of the emirates.

Getting Around

The extraordinary nature, pace, and extent of economic development that has taken place in the UAE owes much of its success to the establishment of a first-class road system. The

Money Facts

The basic unit of currency in the United Arab Emirates is the dirham (Dh). One dirham equals 100 fils. Paper currency is issued in 5-, 10-, 20-, 50-, 100-, 200-, 500-, and 1,000-dirham notes. Coins are issued in 1-dirham, 25-fils, and 50-fils denominations. In April 2001, U.S.$1 equaled 3.71 dirhams.

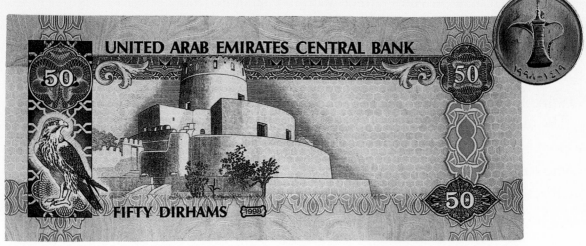

الشــندغة ديرة ديرة
ميناءراشد الراس الشارقة
Al-Shindagha   Deira   Deira
Port Rashid   Al-Ras   Al-Sharjah

highways in the UAE rank as some of the best in the Middle East. Paved roads, many of them multilane expressways, connect every major city.

    The UAE has six international airports serving all corners of the globe. The national airlines are Gulf Air and Emirates Airlines. The governments of Abu Dhabi, Bahrain, Qatar, and Oman own Gulf Air. Emirates Airlines, established in 1985, is

Expressways cross the UAE.

Black Gold   **75**

View of the terminal at Abu Dhabi International Airport

owned by the government of Dubai. It is one of the fastest-growing airlines in the world and has already won several top awards including Airline of the Year. Emirates Airlines recently announced its intent to purchase seven new Airbus A380 superjumbo, double-deck jets. These flying cruise ships are capable of carrying more than 550 passengers. Emirates was the first airline to place an order with Airbus Industries, a European company.

Possessing 168 deepwater berths, the UAE is capable of serving almost half of the entire shipping activity in the Persian (Arabian) Gulf. All seven emirates have coastal access, and each emirate has its own port. Dubai and Sharjah have two ports each. Dubai maintains the largest dry-dock in the Middle East for repairing ships.

The UAE has witnessed one of the most unique economic reversals in world history. Thirty years ago, it could offer little in terms of prosperity to its citizens. Today, UAE citizens enjoy the privileges of a first-class world economy. Their per capita income is one of the highest in the world, and wise leadership has guaranteed them a bright future.

Boats at the harbor in Dubai

Many Different Faces

78

F OR CENTURIES, THE LAND OF THE UNITED ARAB EMIRATES was sparsely populated. In the past, as much as 90 percent of the total land area was uninhabited. Occasionally, migrating Bedouin tribes would pass through an area, but they seldom established permanent settlements. By the middle of the twentieth century, there were no large cities. Only a few small villages existed along the coasts and at the interior oases.

Opposite: **A Muslim woman in Dubai**

Counting Heads

The British conducted the first census in 1968. They determined that about 180,000 people lived in the emirates. This census also indicated that 64 percent of the population were Emiratis, or *nationals*. The other 36 percent were foreigners, or *expatriates*. In 2000, the population was estimated at 2,835,000. The Emiratis now compose only one-quarter of the population, even though their numbers exceed 700,000. The population of foreign residents has increased to more than 2,000,000.

The large gap in numbers between the native Arab population and the

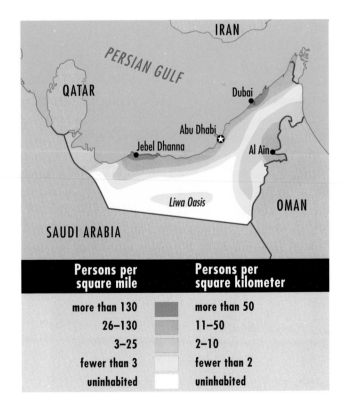

Persons per square mile	Persons per square kilometer
more than 130	more than 50
26–130	11–50
3–25	2–10
fewer than 3	fewer than 2
uninhabited	uninhabited

Who Lives in United Arab Emirates?

Arabs from the United Arab Emirates	12%
Arabs from other countries	13%
Southern Asians (Bangladeshis, Indians, Pakistanis, Sri Lankans)	45%
Iranians	17%
Other Asians and Africans	8%
Europeans and North Americans	5%

multinational foreign population in the UAE is primarily the result of oil. When the export of oil began in 1962, large sums of money began to flow into the country. For the first time, there was ample money to spend on development. Hospitals, roads, schools, airports, ports, and communication networks all became major projects. Workers were needed badly, and the local population could not meet the demand. Foreigners were hired by the hundreds of thousands to help modernize the nation.

Reversing a Trend

A women's clinic

Today, the government is seeking to slow and, where possible, reverse that trend. One way to accomplish this task is to increase the number of nationals. Health care plays a large role in that goal. Currently, there are fifty-one hospitals with 6,357 beds. Almost 1,000 public and private clinics are spread throughout the country. The United Nations recently reported that 99 percent of the population has access to health-care services within an hour's drive of their homes. In addition, the UAE provides its citizens some of the most advanced health care in the world, and it is free.

Since 1960, the results of improved health care have been dramatic. The annual death rate has dropped to less than 2 people per 1,000. Infant mortality rates have decreased from 145 per 1,000 to 16 per 1,000. Life expectancy has risen from fifty-three years to seventy-six years. This remarkable set of accomplishments means that there are more nationals, that their health is better, and that they are living longer.

An old Arab proverb states, "O cousin, do not marry a stranger you meet: our chaff is better than their foreign wheat." In 1994, Sheikh Zayed announced the creation of a new program to boost the percentage of nationals in the total population. The government established a Marriage Fund to encourage UAE men to marry UAE women, rather than women from other countries. Young UAE couples can receive a grant of up to U.S.$19,000 to assist with wedding expenses and buying a house. The grant is interest-free, and the payback rate is less than U.S.$30 per month. To encourage children,

An Arab man and wife in their new home.

Population of Major UAE Cities	
Abu Dhabi	500,000 (1990 est.)
Dubai	400,000 (1990 est.)
Sharjah	320,000 (1987 est.)
Al Ain	176,411 (1989 est.)
Ras al-Khaimah	132,000 (1987 est.)

the couple's debt is reduced by 20 percent with the birth of each child. The birth of five children wipes out the debt completely.

The Arabs

Native Arabs represent a homogeneous group, while the expatriates are multinational and multi-cultural. The overwhelming majority of UAE citizens are of Arab origin. However, in the northern emirates, many citizens have ancestors who came from India, Iran, and Pakistan. The Arabs, in common with Jews, are descendants of the Semitic race, which originated in northwestern Arabia.

The Arabs of the UAE share two common bonds with all other Arabs. One is language and the other is religion. In the UAE, Arabic is the official language and Islam is the official religion. The Arabic language can never be separated from the religion of Islam. The Holy Qur'an is written in classical Arabic. Each day, when hundreds of millions of Muslims say their prayers, they recite them in Arabic. As a result, Arabic can be heard wherever Muslims gather to pray.

A sign reads "Peace Be with You" in Arabic and English.

The Art of Communication

The Arabic language is a part of the Semitic family of languages. Semitic languages originated in the area that

It's All in a Name

In the Arab world, a person's name reflects the genealogy of the father's side of the family. Both male and female children use their father's first name as their middle name. Children of both sexes retain the father's family name. A woman does not change her family name after marriage. If a girl and a boy were children of the same father, their names would appear in the following context.

Father's First Name	Middle Name	Family Name
Hussein	Rashid	al-Mutawa
Son's Name		
Obaid	Hussein	al-Mutawa
Daughter's Name		
Zulikha	Hussein	al-Mutawa

If the same system were used in the United States and Canada, the names would appear as follows:

Father's First Name	Middle Name	Family Name
Donald	Arthur	Langren
Son's Name		
Carl	Donald	Langren
Daughter's Name		
Rebecca	Donald	Langren

Sometimes the name will include the words *ibn* for males and *bint* for females. These are used to indicate the "son of" or "daughter of" the father. In the first example of Arab names listed above, the names would read *Obaid ibn Hussein al-Mutawa* and *Zulikha bint Hussein al-Mutawa*. The family name indicates a large extended family and is the primary source of a person's identity.

is now Palestine and include Hebrew and Aramaic. There are twenty-eight letters in the Arabic alphabet. Arabic writing is read from the right-hand side of the page to the left. This is opposite the English language, which is read from left to right. There is only one form of written Arabic. As a result, Arab schoolchildren do not learn to print first and write in cursive later.

This Malaysian woman works as a lab technician in a research center.

The Expatriates

Expatriates is a word used to describe foreign residents. They include Indian, Pakistani, Iranian, Malaysian, Australian, British, American, German, and many other nationalities. Expatriates speak a range of languages, are followers of assorted religions, and represent a host of unique cultures. They come because of the availability of jobs, and they have families to support in their homelands. They are welcome because they are the labor backbone on which the economy is being built, operated, and maintained.

Noncitizen foreigners make up 75 percent of the UAE population. Their numbers have been increasing steadily since the mid-1960s. Originally, most of them were male, and they worked primarily in the construction industry. Today, the expatriate labor force is employed in almost every part of the economy. The one exception is that nationals fill most government positions. However, many expatriates find government work as consultants, advisors, and project managers.

Indians and Pakistanis represent the largest group of expatriates. The fishing industry is dominated by these two nationalities. Generally, UAE citizens own the boats, and their crews are either Indian or Pakistani. More than 13,000 fishers bring in one-third of the fish caught in the gulf. Fish is popular in the local diet, and local fishing crews provide 100 percent of the domestic consumption.

A Pakistani weaves wire traps used for fishing.

Indians are also the primary shopkeepers in the UAE. They rent their stores from local citizens and sell a wide variety of products. They operate everything from pharmacies, spice shops, auto parts stores, grocery stores, and garment and textile shops to computer stores. Pakistanis are the major labor force in construction. Some jobs they perform include pouring concrete, paving highways, and framing buildings.

There are also substantial numbers of Iranians engaged in commerce, particularly in the port areas. Southeast Asians are heavily represented by Filipinos who work in health care and as domestic household help. Lebanese can be found in a number of occupations, especially in hotel work. Western Europeans and North Americans are associated with the energy industry and technology fields.

Reservations, Please

In the past ten years, increasing numbers of non-nationals are finding jobs in white-collar occupations. Tourism is the prime example. Five-star hotels are sprouting up across the country like the beloved *faqah* mushrooms after a rain. One of the most popular tourist attractions is a resort development 11 miles (18 km) southwest of Dubai. Here, two hotels and an exciting new water park are attracting tourists from around the world. The Burj al-Arab Hotel, shaped like a giant sail and standing 1,053 feet (321 m) high, is the tallest hotel in the Middle East. The Wild Wadi Water Park is a maze of pools, water slides, and exciting rides. Workers at this water park reflect the international nature of the UAE community. There are Australian and South African lifeguards, Malaysian desk clerks, Indian housekeepers, French chefs, and British accountants.

Future Goals

Today, UAE nationals make up about 12 percent of the country's workforce. The government hopes to expand its program of "emiratization"—the placing of UAE nationals in jobs held by expatriates. It is a realistic goal. The UAE has a large population that is under fifteen years of age. As this age group matures and completes its education, its members will begin to enter the job market in ever-increasing numbers. An additional group of highly educated women is also playing an increasingly important role in the UAE economy. The process of emiratization is expected to increase in the coming years.

Opposite: **Tourists enjoy the Wild Wadi Water Park near Dubai.**

The Straight Path

THE UNITED ARAB EMIRATES IS AN ISLAMIC COUNTRY. About 96 percent of the nation's citizens are Muslims. The remaining 4 percent are mainly Christians or Hindus. The UAE Constitution guarantees all people the freedom to worship the faith of their choice.

The earliest archaeological evidence of organized religion in the UAE dates back to before the time of Judaism and Christianity. Religious practices at that time indicate that the inhabitants were nature worshippers. They may have worshipped fire and animals. In Umm al-Qaiwain, the remains of a temple dedicated to a sun god named Shams were uncovered.

Religions of United Arab Emirates (1995)

Sunni Muslim	80%
Shiite Muslim	16%
Others (Christian, Hindu)	4%

Early Christians

A branch of the earliest Christian church settled in Persia (Iran) in the fifth century A.D. This group was referred to as the Nestorians. They chose this name to honor their founder, Nestorius, who was the bishop of Constantinople from 428 to 431.

The Nestorians split from the main body of Christianity in a dispute over the status of Mary. They argued that Mary was not the divine Mother of God. They believed that Mary was simply the human mother of Christ and nothing more. Because their position was considered heresy, they were forced to move to Persia. From Persia, they established sites in modern-day Kuwait, Iraq, Saudi Arabia, and on the island of Sir Bani Yas in the UAE. They built a monastery and a church on the island, sometime during the sixth century A.D. The foundations of these buildings and pieces of decorated plaster revealing Christian crosses were uncovered in 1992.

After Islam arrived in the UAE in A.D. 630, it appears that Christianity and Islam existed side by side for a few decades. Gradually, the Nestorians faded from the area. Today, they practice their beliefs in only a small number of countries. A unique aspect of their worship service is the Holy Sacrament of Communion. They believe that the sacramental bread that they use today is derived from the dough of the bread eaten at Christ's Last Supper with his disciples.

A Way of Life

In 632, a Muslim army suppressed what would be the only major revolt against Islam in southeastern Arabia. The battle

The oldest mosque in the UAE

The Prophet Muhammad

The Prophet Muhammad was born into an influential family of merchants in Mecca, Saudi Arabia, in A.D. 570. According to Muslim tradition, Mecca was the site of an altar built by Adam and destroyed by the great flood of Noah's time. Later, Abraham and his son, Ishmael, are believed to have rebuilt the altar. Currently, the largest mosque in the world surrounds that altar, which is called the *Ka'ba*.

The Prophet Muhammad was a serious man given to meditation. As he grew older, he was offended by how Abraham's altar was being used. The people of Mecca had converted the Ka'ba to a place of pagan worship with many idols. They also placed a growing emphasis on the accumulation of wealth in place of spiritual values. The Prophet spoke out against these abuses.

At the age of forty, the Prophet received his first revelation from God, through the archangel Gabriel.

These revelations continued at periodic intervals for twenty-two years. The Holy Qur'an is the written text of these revelations. When the Prophet began to preach the words of his revelations, the people of Mecca attempted to kill him. He was forced to flee to the city of Medina to escape. This flight, in A.D. 622, is termed the *Hijra* (migration) and marks the beginning of the Islamic calendar.

In Medina, the Prophet's message to return to the teachings of Abraham was openly accepted. Support for the Prophet grew rapidly, and on January 11, 630, the Prophet and his followers returned in triumph to Mecca. The Prophet destroyed the idols in the Ka'ba and ended pagan worship in Arabia. Although he would die just two years later, he was a religious leader who had a profound and lasting impact on much of the world.

occurred at Dibba along the northeastern coast of the UAE. From that day forward, the people of the UAE would base their lives on the Holy Qur'an as revealed to the Prophet Muhammad. The Constitution drafted for the new nation was drawn from the Qur'anic principles. For UAE citizens, Islam is more than a religion—it is a complete guide to living one's life.

The Prophet Muhammad received the revealed faith of Islam in the seventh century A.D. Within a hundred years of his death, the message of Islam had spread over a vast area. It had spread across North Africa, into Spain, and to within a few miles of Paris, France. To the east, Islam expanded along the Indus Valley across northern India, into the Central Asian republics, and on into China. Today, more than 1.2 billion Muslims follow the teachings of the Prophet Muhammad.

Five Pillars

The acceptance of the teachings of the Prophet Muhammad is reflected in the lives of UAE citizens every day. Islam creates a framework for how they live. This framework is based on the Five Pillars of Islam.

The first pillar is *Shahadah*, the profession of faith. It is a short declaration, which every Muslim makes: "There is no god except God and Muhammad is the messenger of God." Conversion to Islam is simple. The convert, in good faith, states the Shahadah, and is welcomed as a follower of Islam.

The Qur'an in classical Arabic script

The second pillar is *Salat*, the recitation of prayers five times each day. The prayers are always recited in Arabic, regardless of the native language of the person praying. The prayers are ritualistic and include verses from the Qur'an. Individuals can also offer personal prayers in their own language if they desire.

The prayers are said at established times. The first prayer is offered at dawn, and others follow at noon, mid-afternoon, sunset, and nightfall. In the UAE, worshippers stop what they are doing to participate in the prayers. If there is a mosque nearby, they participate with other followers in the mosque. However, it is quite acceptable to pray in a factory, a field, an office, a university, or at home. The commitment to daily prayers is one of the first cultural observations that new visitors to the UAE witness.

A Muslim says prayers in a parking lot.

A Place of Worship

A mosque is the central place of worship for Muslims. The mosque is the equivalent of a church or cathedral for Christians or a synagogue for Jews. Mosques can be large, such as the King Faisal Mosque in Sharjah, where 3,000 people can worship. They can also be small, such as those along major highways.

In the UAE, mosques reveal some of the most stunning architectural design in the country. Elaborate arches, domes, and geometric designs produce buildings that are very pleasing to the eye. A tower on the outside of the mosque is termed the *minaret* and is usually the tallest part of the building. Originally, a man known as the *muezzin* gave the call to prayer from the minaret in a strong, melodic voice. Today, the call to prayer is generally played over speakers in the minaret.

The third pillar in Islam is the *Zakat*, or the sharing of one's blessing from God. It is considered to be one of the most important principles of Islam. Each Muslim personally decides how much wealth to share. Donations may be to a mosque, to the Red Crescent Society (the Islamic Red Cross), to a neighbor in need, or to an international relief organization. While giving is a personal decision, 2.5 percent of income is standard in the UAE. Perhaps the best example of Zakat is the one set by the government. The UAE government has contributed billions of dollars of financial assistance to worthy causes. For instance, the country made a major donation to Honduras, to help people in that country recover from a devastating hurricane.

Sawm—fasting during the holy month of Ramadan—is the fourth pillar. In the UAE and around the world, Muslims abstain from food, drink, and sexual relations from sunrise to

Two Calendars

In the Islamic world, people use two calendars. The Muslim lunar calendar consists of a 354-day year. There are twelve months of either twenty-nine or thirty days. As each month begins with the new moon, the study of astronomy has always been important to Muslims. The first year on the Muslim calendar is A.D. 622, which is the year of the Prophet's migration (*Hijra*) to Medina. Letters from Muslim societies frequently list two dates. The year 2000 on the Gregorian (solar) calendar would be AH (After Hijra) 1420–1421 on the Muslim (lunar) calendar. All Islamic holidays are based on the lunar calendar.

UAE citizens also use the Gregorian calendar, which is based on the 365-day revolution of Earth around the sun. This calendar is used for business purposes because of its international acceptance. Because the lunar calendar is eleven days shorter than the solar calendar, Muslim holidays occur on different dates each year. Ramadan, for example, will be celebrated in every season of the year during the course of an average Muslim's life.

sunset during Ramadan. Fasting is viewed as a method of self-purification. It allows the participant to experience the sensations of hunger and thirst. This experience creates sympathy and understanding for those who suffer from hunger and thirst regularly. It is also a time for spiritual growth, personal reflection, and the renewal of family ties.

The fifth and final pillar of Islam is the *Hajj*, a pilgrimage to Mecca. Every devout Muslim will attempt to make the pilgrimage to Mecca once in his or her lifetime. It is an obligation only for those believers who are financially and physically capable of making the trip. Each year, about 2 million people from all over the world assemble in Mecca. Participants describe the experience as the most spiritually rewarding event in their lives.

When pilgrims arrive, they are wearing simple garments that remove all class distinctions. Kings often stand alongside simple peasants. During the Hajj, all are equal before God. Everyone joins the ritual that includes circling the Ka'ba seven times. They also walk seven times between the mountains of Safa and Marwa. The walk commemorates Hagar's search for water in the desert. Hagar was Abraham's concubine and the mother of Ishmael. Muslims believe that they are descendants of Ishmael. On the final day of the

Important Religious (Islamic) Holidays

The following religious holidays are based on the Muslim (lunar) calendar and fall on different dates and in different months according to the Gregorian (solar) calendar used by most nations.

Birthday of the Prophet Muhammad

Ramadan   A month of fasting from dawn to dusk

Eid al-Fitr   The three-day celebration at the end of Ramadan

Eid al-Adha   A four-day celebration after the main pilgrimage to Mecca

Lailat al Mi'raj   Ascension of the Prophet Muhammad

Hajj, the pilgrims gather on the plain of Arafat. Here, they pray for God's forgiveness as a prelude to the day of judgment.

A Living Faith

It would be difficult to overemphasize the role that Islam plays in the daily lives of UAE citizens. Their religion is the glue that holds their families together. Their moral code and behavior reflect their commitment to the principles that the Prophet taught. They abstain from eating pork and do not consume alcohol. The consumption of healthy food and maintenance of a healthy lifestyle are viewed as religious obligations. Children consider it a privilege rather than a responsibility to care for their parents in their old age. Their outlook on life can be summarized in one simple statement, "*In shallah*," meaning, "If it is God's will." They believe that God determines the fate of all humans.

Muslim boys study the Qur'an.

Traditions Old and New

THE PEOPLE OF THE UNITED ARAB EMIRATES REFLECT many of the cultural characteristics found in other parts of the Arab world. They are generous, polite, loyal, and possess a warm sense of humor. Their religion and their families form the central focus of their lives. They have made the transition from a rural desert environment to a largely urban society at breakneck speed. They now live in a world of skyscrapers, cell phones, computers, luxury cars, and open-heart surgery. However, they have not forgotten their past, and they cherish and protect those rich, historical traditions with open enthusiasm.

Opposite: **Boys wearing traditional clothing**

Characteristics of Culture

Some aspects of UAE culture are easy to spot. The country's citizens love children. They believe that wisdom increases with age. They are convinced that the personalities of men and women are, by nature, markedly different. They also believe that those differences should be recognized, celebrated, appreciated, and not be viewed as a source of conflict.

In the UAE, friendships are made easily and quickly. Visits among friends occur frequently, sometimes daily. True friends would not think it a problem to call on one another at any time or for any reason. In fact, in Arabic the closest word to *privacy* means loneliness. Friends give and receive favors freely as part of their relationship.

Emiratis love to talk. Conversation is their most popular form of entertainment. Religion and politics are favorite subjects of discussion. The discussions can become quite emotional, with raised voices, repeated points, interruptions, and waving arms. This is seldom done in anger but instead indicates the sincerity of the speaker.

Men talking in the market

An extended family

Family Roles

An Emirati's family is considered a gift from God. Family loyalty and obligations are more important than other social responsibilities. Tradition guides the family structure. The father is the main wage earner. He is a source of love for his children, but he also has the final say in matters of behavior and discipline. Mothers are the central source of emotional support, and they give structure and meaning to the upbringing of a child. They are kind, patient, and forgiving. In fact, mothers have a greater tendency than fathers to spoil their children, especially their sons.

Mothers are patient and forgiving.

While children are adored by their parents, they are also expected to behave in an appropriate manner. It is especially important that children mind their manners in the presence of adults. A good child should never interrupt or talk back to an adult. Children are taught to feel shame instead of guilt. An important goal is to avoid bringing shame to one's family at all costs.

Dating and marriage customs in the UAE differ greatly from Western customs. Young men and women usually do not go out on dates before getting married. There is no physical contact or kissing. Abstinence is practiced prior to marriage. Even after marriage, public displays of affection are not acceptable.

The concept of romance or falling in love is not a part of UAE life. Families usually arrange marriages between their sons and daughters. They believe that marriage should provide

A bride prepares for her wedding.

financial security, social status, and the opportunity to raise children in the most positive and healthy environment. In most situations, couples develop a deep affection for each other over time. The divorce rate for marriages in the UAE is much lower than the divorce rates in the United States and Canada.

Women in Society

The role of women in the UAE has changed dramatically since independence in 1971. Education has been the springboard for many young women to enter professional careers. Currently, 98 percent of all females eligible to go to school are attending school. In numbers, they dominate their male counterparts at every level of education from kindergarten through university. Women make up 60 percent of the student body at the UAE University in Al Ain. About 70 percent of the students at the Higher Colleges of Technology are women.

Women dominate the teaching field and health services while accounting

Female students at the UAE University

Paradise Gained

If possible, a dying Muslim will whisper the *Shahadah* (profession of faith) with his or her last breath. The soul departs at the moment of death for eternal life in paradise. After death, the body is washed, usually by a family member, and wrapped in white cloth. Family and friends carry the deceased to the cemetery while chanting the Shahadah. The body is placed in the grave with the right side facing Mecca. If possible, the burial will take place before sundown on the day of death. The grave will be marked with a slab of rock. Elaborate monuments are not erected in Muslim cemeteries, and outsiders seldom notice the cemeteries.

for 40 percent of all government employees. The Faculty of Medicine and Health Sciences at the UAE University in Al Ain is currently training several female doctors. The UAE's first woman pilot recently graduated from Dubai Aviation College. Most remarkable of all are the hundreds of young UAE women who serve in various military positions with the exception of combat. Twenty years ago, these accomplishments would have been inconceivable.

Many of these changes are the result of the UAE Women's Federation. The federation was established in 1975 under the leadership of H.H. Sheikha Fatima bint Mubarak, wife of UAE president Sheikh Zayed. The federation is composed of six major groups with thirty-one branches, serving all areas of the country.

The organization receives funding from the federal government. It has its own charter and the authority to enter into discussions with ministries and government departments. The federation can also suggest new laws or amendments to existing laws. It has used its authority wisely in representing the interests of women.

Al Husn Palace

Al Husn Palace, sometimes called the White Fort, is located in the city center of Abu Dhabi. The original fort was constructed in 1793, over a freshwater well. The present fort was built in the late nineteenth century and once served as the residence of the ruler of Abu Dhabi. It is the oldest building in Abu Dhabi. All other buildings in the city were built after 1950. The Document and Research Center is housed in Al Husn Palace. This center has been recognized internationally for its work on historical documentation in the Persian (Arabian) Gulf region.

A Place to Learn

The Cultural Foundation in Abu Dhabi is the national center for cultural events, historical documents, and research. The complex occupies 35 acres (14 ha) and includes the National Library, the Institution of Culture and Art, Al Husn Palace, and the National Archives.

The Cultural Foundation sponsors many programs to enrich the lives of children. The foundation offers courses in computer literacy, painting, sculpture, music, ballet, theater, Arabic calligraphy, and recitation and memorization of the Holy Qur'an. It conducts field trips to important historical sites and organizes an annual children's festival. The foundation also publishes a magazine written and illustrated by children.

Traditional music and dance continue to play an important role in the lives of UAE citizens. Native dancers and musicians regularly perform on national holidays and at wedding celebrations. The music is created with multiple drums of different sizes and tones. Sometimes a tambourine is added to liven the presentation. There is almost always a wind instrument, called an Arabian flute (*nai*), which produces a sad, haunting melody. Finally, a string instrument called a *rababa* is used to accompany singers.

A traditional music group features drums.

Men perform the ayyala with wooden canes.

The songs reflect the past. Sometimes they tell a story of what life was like in the villages. Songs about the sea were originally performed on pearling ships. There was a special song for each task on the boat. Song were created for lifting the anchor, raising the mainsail, and diving for pearls. The Bedouins also had songs that are called desert songs. One song, the *Hida'a*, was sung to relax the camels on long desert journeys.

The dance that is most identified with UAE tradition is the *ayyala*. During this dance, rows of men holding swords or sticks move backward and forward toward each other to the beat of drums. It creates the image of a battle between the two groups. Female dancers perform a dance known as the *na'ashat*. They place their right hand on their chest and sway slowly from one side to the other. As they go through this motion, their long black hair sways from side to side, creating a hypnotic effect.

Camel Racing

Superhighways and large trucks have replaced camels as the major means of transporting goods. However, camels are still held in high esteem and have become a popular source of entertainment. Informal camel races of the past have evolved into competitions held at major racetracks around the country.

The races are conducted during the winter months when it is cooler. Most of the racetracks are 5–7 miles (8–11 km) long. On race day, the grounds around the track are filled with spectators. Coffee and tea are brewed over open fires and the aroma of shish kabobs fills the air. The event has the atmosphere of a tailgate party at a U.S. football game. Chaos breaks out at the beginning of the race as jockeys maneuver for the lead position. The spectators honk their horns, wave their arms, and cheer wildly for their favorites.

Young boys are the jockeys in some camel races.

The camels can reach speeds of 12 miles per hour (more than 19 kph). The owner of the winning camel may win thousands of dollars in prizes, including a luxury automobile. A top-level racing camel can sell for U.S.$1 million.

A Proud Bird

Many men in the UAE enjoy returning to the desert to practice the ancient sport of falconry. Using trained falcons, they stalk their favorite prey, the houbara bustard. The houbara is a much larger bird than the falcon, standing up to 30 inches (76 cm) tall and weighing as much as 9 pounds (4 kilograms). Although the houbara is powerful and fast, it is no match for the blazing speed of the falcon or its razor-sharp talons. Even when the hunt is not successful, the time spent with friends in the desert is very special.

Falconry is an ancient tradition in the UAE.

Bred for Speed

The Arabian horse is an animal of considerable grace and strength. The Bedouins have bred Arabian horses for centuries. Historically, they were used to ride into battle. Now, they are bred for competitive horse racing. Every Thoroughbred race-horse that competes today is a descendant of one of three Arabian stallions. Sheikh Zayed is the registered owner of the largest number of Arabian horses in the world.

Arabian horses are popular in the UAE and around the world.

The Dubai World Cup

The horse race known as the Dubai World Cup has gained international fame. Offering a multimillion-dollar purse to the winner, the race has become the richest horse race in the world. When the Dubai World Cup was first run in 1996, world television was focused on the event. A horse named Cigar was flown 6,000 miles (9,656 km) from the United States to run against the top horses. Cigar won the race at the wire, completing his thirteenth consecutive win.

A Goal in Mind

Soccer, which is called football in the UAE, is the most popular sport. It is played from grade school through college. At the national level, there are twenty-six soccer clubs, each averaging 150 players. Although it is a small country, the UAE national team played in the World Cup finals held in Italy in 1990. In the 1996–1997 season, the UAE team competed against Saudi Arabia for the Asian Cup Football Championship.

Up to Par

Golf has become the fastest-growing sport in the country. Players have their choice of several world-class courses. Interest in golf skyrocketed after the first grass championship course in the gulf was built in Dubai. The Emirates Golf Club soon attracted the attention of international golfers. In 1989, the Dubai Desert Classic became an official tournament on the PGA European Tour. Since then, the tournament has been won by some of the best-known golfers in the world. Winners include Seve Ballesteros and José María Olazabal of Spain, Ernie Els of South Africa, Colin Montgomerie of Scotland, and Fred Couples of the United States. In 2001, Thomas Bjorn of Denmark won the Dubai Desert Classic. Tiger Woods, probably the best golfer in the world, took a double bogey on the final hole and tied for second place.

The Fastest Arab on Wheels

Motorcar rally racing is one of the most challenging of all automotive sports. It pits car and driver against the elements of nature. The race is an off-road event that requires extraordinary endurance from the car and the driver. Some races are more than 1,243 miles (2,000 km) through the desert. One man dominates this sport in the Middle East. UAE national Mohammed bin Sulayem has captured nearly fifty international titles. He has won the Middle East Championship ten times. This success has earned him the title "The Fastest Arab on Wheels."

Life Is Good

An elegant home on
Jumeirah Beach

DAILY LIFE IN THE UNITED ARAB EMIRATES HAS CHANGED
dramatically over the past three decades. The country is no
longer isolated from the rest of the world. Business and government leaders operate on a global scale. The pace and
diversity of life for families has also increased. Still, some areas
of daily life reveal little change over the centuries.

Opposite: **Gold jewelry
glitters in a shop window.**

A Place to Live

One of the most dramatic changes is evident in the development of modern housing. Very few people still live in
mud-brick homes or structures made of palm fronds. The government has built more than 50,000 modern houses in rural
areas. The houses are provided to citizens free of charge. In
the cities, the government provides low-interest loans so that
people can build their dream homes. Elegant houses create an
urban scene that is visually stimulating. Well-trimmed lawns,

flower gardens, and stately palm trees add to the beauty. Electricity and water from desalination plants are provided to citizens free or at a very low cost.

A Place to Study

In 1950, there were no public schools in the United Arab Emirates. There were only a few mosque schools, in which boys were taught to memorize and recite the Holy Qur'an. The first public school was established in Sharjah in 1953. By 1972, primary education was required of all children. Today, the UAE has a modern educational system that has reduced the rate of illiteracy to less than 20 percent. Students can attend school from kindergarten through college at no cost.

Girls and boys go to different schools. However, the courses they study are very similar. Religion classes are taught at all

Students at a primary school

levels of education. There is no separation of church and state in the UAE, because Islam is an all-encompassing way of life.

A student studying computer science

The UAE University in Al Ain opened in 1977. In 1998, about 15,000 students attended the university. The Higher Colleges of Technology (HCT) were established in 1988 with about 289 students. Today, the HCT have ten campuses with a combined enrollment of almost 10,000 students. These schools provide some of the most advanced technological training in the Middle East. Businesses frequently try to hire students before they graduate from these esteemed universities.

National Holidays in the United Arab Emirates

New Year's Day	January 1
National Day	December 2

Time to Work

The work week in the UAE begins on Saturday and normally ends at noon on Thursday. Friday is the day of worship in the Muslim world. On workdays, government offices open at 7:00 or 7:30 A.M. They close at 1:00 or 1:30 P.M., creating a six-hour workday. Businesses open at 8:00 or 8:30 A.M., take a three-hour break at midday, and close at 7:00 or 8:00 P.M. These schedules allow employees to avoid working in the high heat of the early afternoon.

Foreigners conducting business in the UAE will find that business meetings almost always open with an invitation for coffee or tea and some light conversation. Western businesspeople who want to rush negotiations may lose a contract because of their impatience.

A technician working in a music studio

Taxi, Please

In Dubai, a major waterway, known fondly as the Creek, separates the old city from the new commercial district. Traditional boats called *abras* ferry passengers from one side of the waterway to the other. Although two bridges and a tunnel also cross the Creek, it is a lot more fun to take the water taxi.

The Road to Work

The United Arab Emirates has a superb road network. Since most cities have been thoroughly modernized over the past quarter-century, the main streets are multilane, divided boulevards. Many Emiratis own large luxury cars. In the cities they are permitted to drive 37 miles per hour (60 kph), and in the countryside they can drive 62 miles per hour (100 kph). The police use clever techniques to discourage speeders. They disguise cameras in the bushes to record the car's speed and license plate. A few days later, offending speeders usually receive letters informing them of the fines they must pay.

Arab and American guests sit at a traditional dinner.

The Joy of Food

Even with the hectic pace of life today, most families manage to eat their midday or evening meal together. Meals are eaten in the traditional manner. Several platters of food are placed on a clean

The Good Host

Hospitality is an Arab tradition. One of the cherished rituals of being a good host is to offer your guest coffee or tea. Coffee beans, chosen preferably from Yemen due to their rich flavor, are fresh-roasted each day. The beans are ground into a fine powder. The ground coffee is brought to a boil two or three times in a large pot. Frequently, cardamom is added to give the coffee a distinct flavor. The coffee is poured from a brass pot into small porcelain cups provided by the server. The server fills one-third to one-half of the cup. After drinking the coffee, a guest holds the cup in the air with the right hand if desiring more coffee. If the guest wants no more coffee, the cup is lifted and shaken slightly from one side to the other.

plastic mat on the floor of the eating room. Members of the family sit around the mat with their legs crossed beneath them. Food is passed and eaten with the right hand. Eating utensils are not used. A child learns at an early age how to pick up food, even rice, with the right hand.

A good cook is much admired in the UAE. Eating is something of a national pastime, and everyone appreciates food that has been well prepared. Most foods are prepared using a variety of spices, which enrich the flavor. One of the most popular stores in the market is the spice shop.

Let's Eat

Breakfast is usually a light meal with coffee and dates. On occasion, pasta made from eggs, onions, cinnamon, sugar, and oil (*al-balaleef*) is served. Lunch is a feast. There will always be a major meat dish, commonly fish or lamb, served with rice. Several side dishes such as *hummus* (chickpeas and sesame paste), *tabbouleh* (bulghur wheat with mint and parsley), and *warak enab* (stuffed grape leaves) are prepared. Arab flat bread is used to soak up meat juice or dip in the side dishes. Desserts are always offered with coffee or tea to top off the meal. *Al halwa* is one of the most popular sweets. It is made from sugar, eggs, starch, water, and oil. The cook does not spare the sugar.

No one leaves an Arab meal hungry. In the evenings, dinner can consist of anything from leftovers to fast food or even a main course.

Shops that sell gold are
found in every city.

Perfume and Jewelry

Women of the UAE enjoy shopping for perfume or jewelry. Arab women have used aromatic oils and perfumes since pre-Islamic times. They frequently mix their own ingredients. Sandalwood, saffron, amber, and musk are favorites. In order to obtain the right fragrance, they will sometimes add extracts of the flowers of jasmine, narcissus, or lilies.

In Bedouin days, a woman's wealth was measured by her jewelry collection. Handmade silver jewelry and amber beads were cherished. Gold is the choice of today's women. Every city has a gold souq with beautiful collections of 21- and 23-carat gold jewelry for sale. Gold jewelry is popular throughout the Arab world, and Dubai is the gold capital. More than 20 percent of the world's annual gold production moves through Dubai. Mothers teach their daughters how to shop for gold at an early age.

Dressing in Style

Fashion has changed little since the modern era arrived in the UAE. Both men and women dress conservatively as part of their heritage. They are shocked at the Western world's tendency to allow men and women to expose so much of the human body.

Men wear a traditional garment called a *dishdasha* or *kandura*. It is usually made from cotton and is white or light-colored to reflect the rays of the sun. It slips on over the shoulders and covers the man's body from his neck to his ankles. The garment is loose fitting and allows air to move

Men in traditional clothing

about freely underneath. It is the perfect choice for comfort in a hot, desert environment.

Most men wear a traditional headdress that is composed of three pieces. The first is the *qahfiyya*, a small flat skullcap that fits tightly over the scalp. The *ghutra* is a large piece of white or red-checkered cloth. It is folded into a triangle and placed over the qahfiyya. The *agal* is a black, ropelike cord with a circular shape that fits tightly around the crown of the head. The agal prevents the ghutra from shifting or blowing off in the wind.

Women's clothes are made from brightly patterned fabrics. Red, green, yellow, and blue are popular colors, and many garments are embroidered with gold and silver thread. A loose fitting, trouserlike garment called the *sirwai* reaches from the waist to the ankles. The *dara'a*, or dress, is the next layer of clothing. It is made from silk or cotton and is very elegant. The *abbaya*, a black cloaklike wrap, is worn on the outside. Over her head, a woman may wear a *shaileh*. It has the appearance of a scarf, covers her hair, and is tucked in below the chin. Older women may wear a veil across their face. Many women wear a mask instead of a veil, and veiling is becoming less common.

Schoolchildren dress in Western or traditional Arab clothes. Even if they select Western styles, they still dress conservatively. Long pants, long-sleeved shirts or blouses, and appropriate hairstyles are acceptable at school.

A woman in traditional veil and abbaya

Traditional Games

Al-labeeda is a game played all over the world. In the United States and Canada it is known as hide-and-seek. *Al-karaba* involves two players. Each player holds one leg in his hand while hopping on the other leg. The player who is able to knock the other player down wins the game. In *al-saqla*, two to four players compete against each other. Each player has five smooth pebbles. Four pebbles are placed on the ground. The fifth pebble is tossed into the air. The trick is to pick up each of the other four pebbles one at a time before the fifth pebble hits the ground. The game requires speed, accuracy, and great eye-hand coordination.

Playtime

One measure for judging the wealth of a nation is the number and cost of children's toys. Children of the UAE differ little from American and Canadian children. Many have the latest Nintendo and Sega games. If they can, they buy all of the new battery-operated gizmos and lounge in their rooms with headphones connected to CD players. Television is rapidly becoming a favorite pastime, which is a matter of concern for parents.

It is difficult for young citizens of the UAE to imagine the hardships that their parents and grandparents faced. The country is a far different place to live in than it was fifty years ago. Desert is no longer the best word to describe the United Arab Emirates. Dynamic would be a more appropriate word. It is a nation with a very bright future.

Opposite: **This scene at Dubai's Creek shows modern skyscrapers.**

Timeline

United Arab Emirates History		World History	
Traders are living in what is now the United Arab Emirates.	3000 B.C.		
Umm al-Nar culture of fishers and farmers develops.	2500–2000 B.C.	2500 B.C.	Egyptians build the Pyramids and the Sphinx in Giza.
Camels are domesticated and *falaj* irrigation system is developed.	1200–300 B.C.	563 B.C.	The Buddha is born in India.
		A.D. 313	The Roman emperor Constantine recognizes Christianity.
Islamic religion spreads throughout what is now the UAE.	A.D. 630s	610	The Prophet Muhammad begins preaching a new religion called Islam.
		1054	The Eastern (Orthodox) and Western (Roman) Churches break apart.
		1066	William the Conqueror defeats the English in the Battle of Hastings.
		1095	Pope Urban II proclaims the First Crusade.
		1215	King John seals the Magna Carta.
		1300s	The Renaissance begins in Italy.
		1347	The Black Death sweeps through Europe.
		1453	Ottoman Turks capture Constantinople, conquering the Byzantine Empire.
		1492	Columbus arrives in North America.
Portuguese traders take over trade in the area.	1500s	1500s	The Reformation leads to the birth of Protestantism.
Ras al-Khaimah and Sharjah begin to develop as strong states.	1700s	1776	The Declaration of Independence is signed.
British forces destroy the city of Ras al-Khaimah; sheikhs of the seven Trucial States sign a peace treaty with the British government.	1820	1789	The French Revolution begins.
British promise to protect the area from attacks by other people.	1853		
Sheikhs agree that they will deal with no foreign governments other than Great Britain.	1892	1865	The American Civil War ends.

United Arab Emirates History

Abu Dhabi and Dubai are the leading states.	**Early 1900s**
Oil is discovered in Abu Dhabi.	**1959**
Oil is discovered in Dubai.	**1966**
Britain agrees to leave the Persian (Arabian) Gulf; sheikhs of the emirates work out a way to form a federation.	**1968–1971**
The United Arab Emirates is formed by Abu Dhabi, Dubai, Sharjah, Ajman, Umm al-Qaiwain, and Fujairah.	**1971**
Ras al-Khaimah is the seventh emirate to join the UAE.	**1972**
The UAE and other Arab countries form the Gulf Cooperative Council.	**1981**
Dubai Desert Classic becomes a golf tournament on the PGA European Tour.	**1989**
The UAE takes part in the Gulf War against Iraq.	**1991**
The Dubai World Cup horse race is run for the first time.	**1996**
The UAE pays almost $8 billion for 80 fighter jets and missiles from a U.S. company.	**2000**

World History

1914	World War I breaks out.
1917	The Bolshevik Revolution brings communism to Russia.
1929	Worldwide economic depression begins.
1939	World War II begins, following the German invasion of Poland.
1945	World War II ends.
1957	The Vietnam War starts.
1969	Humans land on the moon.
1975	The Vietnam War ends.
1979	Soviet Union invades Afghanistan.
1983	Drought and famine in Africa.
1989	The Berlin Wall is torn down, as communism crumbles in Eastern Europe.
1991	Soviet Union breaks into separate states.
1992	Bill Clinton is elected U.S. president.
2000	George W. Bush is elected U.S. president.

Fast Facts

Official name: United Arab Emirates (composed of Abu Dhabi, Dubai, Sharjah, Ras al-Khaimah, Umm al-Qaiwain, Ajman, and Fujairah)

Capital: Abu Dhabi

Dubai

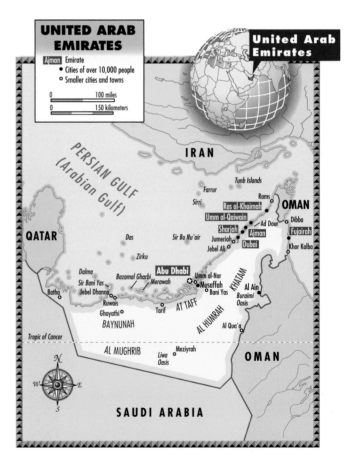

Flag of the United
Arab Emirates

Official language:	Arabic
Official religion:	Islam
Year of founding:	1971
Government:	Federation
Chief of state:	President
Head of government:	Supreme Council of Rulers
Area and dimensions:	32,280 square miles (83,600 sq km); 250 miles (402 km) north to south; 350 miles (563 km) east to west
Latitude and longitude of geographic center:	24° N, 54° E
Borders:	Persian (Arabian) Gulf to the north; Oman to the northeast and east; Gulf of Oman to the east; Saudi Arabia to the south and west; Qatar to the west
Highest elevation:	Jebel Yibir in the Hajar Mountains, 5,010 feet (1,527 m) above sea level
Lowest elevation:	Salamiyah, a salt flat, slightly below sea level
Highest average temperature:	120°F (49°C) in the desert in the summer
Lowest average temperature:	65°F (18°C) in the winter
National population (2000 est.):	2,835,000

Hajar Mountains

A fort on the Persian Gulf

Currency

Population of largest cities:

Abu Dhabi	500,000 (1990 est.)
Dubai	400,000 (1990 est.)
Sharjah	320,000 (1987 est.)
Al Ain	176,411 (1989 est.)
Ras al-Khaimah	132,000 (1987 est.)

Famous landmarks:

▶ *Al-Hosn Palace*, Abu Dhabi

▶ *Hajar Mountains*

▶ *Heritage Area*, Sharjah

▶ *Khor Kalba*, nature reserve in Fujairah

▶ *King Faisal Mosque*, Sharjah

▶ *Liwa Oasis*, Abu Dhabi

▶ *Old Souq*, market in Abu Dhabi

▶ *Sir Bani Yas Island*, Abu Dhabi

Industry: Oil is the United Arab Emirates' most important product, and the UAE makes most of its income from exporting crude oil. The Emirates of Abu Dhabi, Dubai, and Sharjah are the largest producers. In recent years, the country has built refineries that process some of the oil. The country also makes much money producing and exporting natural gas. Other areas of trade include exporting dates and fish and importing building supplies, machinery, and consumer goods such as clothing and food products.

Currency: The UAE dirham (Dh) is the basic monetary unit. 1 Dh=100 fils; U.S.$1 = 3.71 Dh (April 2001).

System of weights and measures: Metric system

Literacy (1995): 79 percent

Boys in traditional clothing

Common Arabic words and phrases:

As-salaamu alaykum.	Hello.
Ma'al salaama.	Good-bye.
Shukran.	Thank you.
Afwan.	You're welcome.
ayyawa	yes
la'	no
As-sa a kam?	What time is it?
Ana min kanad /amrika.	I'm from Canada/ the USA.
Fursa sa'ida.	Pleased to meet you.
Ismi . . .	My name is . . .
khubz	bread
Maf mushkila.	No problem.
mayya	water
qahwa	coffee
Sabah al-kheir.	Good morning.

Famous Emiratis:

Ahmed bin Majid
15th-century geographer and explorer

Sheikh Zayed bin Mohammed
(Zayed the Great)
Ruler of Abu Dhabi, 1855–1909

Sheikh Zayed bin Sultan al-Nahyan
President of the UAE, 1971–present

Sheikha Fatima bint Mubarak
(Wife of President Zayed)
Founder and leader of UAE Women's Federation

Mohammed bin Sulayem
Race-car driver

Sheikh Rashid bin Saeed al-Maktoum
Leader of Dubai, 1958–1990

Supreme Council of Rulers

To Find Out More

Books

► Macdonald, Fiona. *The World of Islam up to 1500s*. London, U.K.: Collins Educational, 1991.

► Mokhtar, Moktefi. *The Arabs in the Golden Age*. Brookfield, Conn.: Milbrook Press, 1996.

► Waterlow, Julia. *The Red Sea and the Arabian Gulf*. Austin, Tex.: Raintree/Steck Vaughn, 1997.

Websites

► **United Arab Emirates Center**
http://www.ecssr.ac.ae/01uae.homepage.html
Produced by the Emirates Center for Strategic Studies and Research, this is an excellent source of up-to-date material on the United Arab Emirates.

There are maps, addresses, fax numbers, and websites for all of the major government agencies.

► **United Arab Emirates**
http://www.uae-pages.com/
This UAE website is full of information including superb photos illustrating a wide range of cultural and physical features in the country.

Arabia

► http://www.planetarabia.com/main.cfm
This site provides enough cultural opportunities to keep students busy for several days. It offers a wide variety of information and some good activities including games, crossword puzzles, books, music, history, etc. Type in any Arab name and discover what it means.

▶ **About Geography**
http://www.geography.about.com/
science/geography/library/maps/
bluae.htm
*A very good site for maps, flags, and
lots of general information about the
country.*

▶ **Women in the Third World**
http://women3rdworld.about.com/
newsissues/women3rdworld/
msub56.htm
*Marriage customs and practices includ-
ing the description of a wedding
ceremony in the United Arab
Emirates.*

▶ **Jumeirah Beach**
http://www.jumeirah-beach.com/
page12.html
*This fun site for both kids and adults
has superb photography and videos that
illustrate the modern side of tourism in
the UAE.*

▶ **Gulf News**
http://www.gulf-news.co.ae/
17082000/index.htm
*A good site for student research
projects, Gulf News is a very readable
newspaper published in the UAE. It is*

*an excellent source for major stories in
the region as well as photos, weather,
sports, recipes, and the times for the
five daily prayers.*

Posters

▶ **Hajj**
Pictorial Charts Educational Trust
27 Kirchen Road
London UK, W13 OUD
*Catalog No. E 21 Hajj. This poster
explains the concept of Hajj with stunning photography and oral descriptions
of all of the major Hajj experiences. It
is a valuable classroom tool for teaching
about Islam or the Arab world.*

Embassy

▶ **Embassy of the United
Arab Emirates**
Suite 700
1255 22nd Street, N.W
Washington, DC 20037
(202) 955-4502

Index

Page numbers in *italics* indicate illustrations.

Meet the Author

Byron Augustin is a professor of geography at Southwest Texas State University in San Marcos, Texas. His love for geography has instilled in him a passion for traveling abroad whenever he has an opportunity to do so. He has visited forty-nine of the fifty United States, twenty-six of Mexico's thirty-one states, and eight Canadian provinces. Dr. Augustin has visited fifty-four countries on five of the seven continents.

Dr. Augustin is an avid professional photographer. More than 1,000 of his photos have been published worldwide. The National Geographic Society, *Encyclopedia Britannica*, *Outdoor Life*, and scores of books and magazines have published his photographs. More than a dozen books in the Enchantment of the World series feature his photos. He is the author of *Bolivia*, and he and his wife, Rebecca, co-authored *Qatar*, both in the Enchantment of the World series.

Dr. Augustin ranks writing the book on the United Arab Emirates, which he first visited as a National Council on U.S.–Arab Relations Malone Fellow on Arab and Islamic Studies, as among his most enjoyable experiences. He teaches

a course on the geography of North Africa and the Middle East. He has been reading about and conducting research on the Arabian Peninsula for more than ten years. To write this book, he used the superb facilities of his university's library. He also surfed the Internet for several excellent sources of information. Most of his statistical data was provided by government agencies in the United Arab Emirates.

Dr. Augustin believes that it is difficult—if not impossible—to write about a country fairly and accurately without visiting it personally. As a result, he has visited the UAE four times since 1995. In December 1999, he spent two weeks there gathering data, interviewing Emiratis, and taking pictures for the book. He traveled to all seven emirates. He dipped his toes in both the Gulf of Oman and the Persian (Arabian) Gulf. He flew with the UAE Air Force to Sir Bani Yas Island to view its spectacular wildlife restoration preserve. He broke the fast (Iftar) of Ramadan with H.E. Sheikh Nahyan bin Mabarak al-Nahyan at his majlis. From 1990 to 1997, Dr. Augustin served as executive director of the Texas Committee on U.S.–Arab Relations, an affiliate of the Washington, D.C.-based National Council on U.S.–Arab Relations.

Photo Credits